and Lessons

1-15-14

AARON AND MISSY,

THANKS SO MUCH FOR
SHOWING THE LOVE
OF JESUS!
3 JOHN 2.

Jim

Jesus:
His Life
and Lessons

Compiled by
James N. Watkins

Foreword by
Mary DeMuth

Contents

Foreword

When I was twelve years old, I knew very little of Jesus. When I was thirteen, I considered taking my life. These kinds of thoughts haunted me for the next two years. I wondered why in the world I was on this crazy earth and what kind of purpose I had here.

At fourteen, a friend invited me to hear about Jesus. In a meeting crammed with teens, an adult stood up and shared from the Bible about Jesus: what he said, who he talked to, how he acted. When I heard his words for the first time in that context, my heart stirred. With a word, he quieted stormy seas. With a prayer, he fed thousands. With a touch, he healed a leper.

I needed this Jesus.

I continued to hear about Jesus. I placed myself in each story, wondering if he would want to interact with me. Eventually, I heard the entire story of Jesus, including his horrific death because of our sin and his unusual and amazing resurrection.

I had been a fatherless girl, then, longing for stability and love. Jesus offered both. And I've never, ever been the same again. His words, his actions, his life have utterly changed me. I pray he opens your eyes too, as you read his words and sense his great affection for you.

Mary DeMuth, author of *The Wall Around Your Heart: How Jesus Heals Us when Others Hurt Us*

Introduction

The task of creating a chronological narrative of Jesus' life and a topical arrangement of his lessons is a bit like trying to create one giant jigsaw puzzle picture from four smaller jigsaw puzzle pictures. The subject is common to all four gospels—the life and lessons of Jesus—but the individual pieces from his followers, Matthew, Mark, Luke, and John, don't always fit snuggly together on one plane. Some stack on top of each other, others sideways, creating a three-dimensional picture. And John concludes his gospel by mentioning there are many missing pieces in the written record of Jesus' life. But ultimately, the pieces we have provide a consistent, multi-dimensional picture of Jesus.

My goal is to simply provide a general story line of Jesus in the gospel writers' own words and to categorize the actual words of Jesus by topics without any commentary or doctrinal bias. I trust this will be a helpful tool for seekers, new believers, and students of Jesus from all faith backgrounds as we sort through the pieces to get the big picture of Jesus' life and lessons.

Any text appearing in [brackets] is not in the *World English Version,* but is to provide a transition or an explanation. To learn about the process of compiling *Jesus: His Life and Lessons,* see Notes at the back of the book. Also, a Glossary is provided for unique words in the biblical text.

I trust you will discover the God of love who "became human and made his home among us. He was full of unfailing love and faithfulness" (John 1:14).

James N. Watkins
www.jameswatkins.com

Jesus: His Life

Introduction

Since many have undertaken to set in order a narrative concerning those matters which have been fulfilled among us, even as those who from the beginning were eyewitnesses and servants of the word delivered them to us, it seemed good to me also, having traced the course of all things accurately from the first, to write to you in order . . . that you might know the certainty concerning the things in which you were instructed (Luke 1:1-4).

Jesus is God from eternity

In the beginning was the Word, and the Word was with God, and the Word was God. The same was in the beginning with God. All things were made through him. Without him was not anything made that has been made. In him was life, and the life was the light of men. The light shines in the darkness, and the darkness hasn't overcome it.

The Word became flesh, and lived among us. We saw his glory, such glory as of the one and only Son of the Father, full of grace and truth (John 1:1-5, 14).

Birth of Jesus foretold to Mary

Now in the sixth month, the angel Gabriel was sent from God to a city of Galilee, named Nazareth, to a virgin pledged to be married to a man whose name was Joseph, of David's house. [See Jesus' earthly family tree at the end of this section.]

The virgin's name was Mary. Having come in, the angel said to her, "Rejoice, you highly favored one! The Lord is with you. Blessed are you among women!"

But when she saw him, she was greatly troubled at the saying, and considered what kind of salutation this might be. The angel said to her, "Don't be afraid, Mary, for you have found favor with God. Behold, you will conceive in your womb, and give birth to a son, and will call his name 'Jesus.' He will be great, and will be called the Son of the Most High. The Lord God will give him the throne of his father, David, and he will reign over the house of Jacob forever. There will be no end to his Kingdom."

Mary said to the angel, "How can this be, seeing I am a virgin?"

The angel answered her, "The Holy Spirit will come on you, and the power of the Most High will overshadow you. Therefore also the holy one who is born from you will be called the Son of God. Behold, Elizabeth, your relative, also has conceived a son in her old age; and this is the sixth month with her who was called barren. For nothing spoken by God is impossible."

Mary said, "Behold, the servant of the Lord; let it be done to me according to your word."

The angel departed from her. Mary arose in those days and went into the hill country with haste, into a city of Judah, and entered into the house of Zacharias and greeted Elizabeth. When Elizabeth heard Mary's greeting, the baby leaped in her womb, and Elizabeth was filled with the Holy Spirit. She called out with a loud voice, and said, "Blessed are you among women, and blessed is the fruit of your womb! Why am I so favored, that the mother of my Lord should come to me? For behold, when the voice of your greeting came into my ears, the baby leaped in my womb for joy! Blessed is she who believed, for there will be a fulfillment of the things which have been spoken to her from the Lord!"

Mary said,

"My soul magnifies the Lord.
My spirit has rejoiced in God my Savior,
for he has looked at the humble state of his servant.
For behold, from now on, all generations will call me blessed.
For he who is mighty has done great things for me.
Holy is his name.
His mercy is for generations of generations on those who fear

him.
He has shown strength with his arm.
He has scattered the proud in the imagination of their hearts.
He has put down princes from their thrones.
And has exalted the lowly.
He has filled the hungry with good things.
He has sent the rich away empty.
He has given help to Israel, his servant, that he might remember mercy,
As he spoke to our fathers,
to Abraham and his offspring forever."

Mary stayed with her about three months, and then returned to her house (Luke 2:26-56).

Birth of Jesus foretold to Joseph
Joseph, her husband, being a righteous man, and not willing to make [Mary] a public example, intended to put her away secretly. But when he thought about these things, behold, an angel of the Lord appeared to him in a dream, saying, "Joseph, son of David, don't be afraid to take to yourself Mary, your wife, for that which is conceived in her is of the Holy Spirit. She shall give birth to a son. You shall call his name Jesus, for it is he who shall save his people from their sins."

Now all this has happened, that it might be fulfilled which was spoken by the Lord through the prophet, saying,

"Behold, the virgin shall be with child,
and shall give birth to a son.
They shall call his name Immanuel;"
which is, being interpreted, "God with us."

Joseph arose from his sleep, and did as the angel of the Lord commanded him, and took his wife to himself; and didn't know her sexually until she had given birth to her firstborn son (Matthew 1:19-25).

Jesus born in Bethlehem

Now in those days, a decree went out from Caesar Augustus that all the world should be enrolled. This was the first enrollment made when Quirinius was governor of Syria. All went to enroll themselves, everyone to his own city. Joseph also went up from Galilee, out of the city of Nazareth, into Judea, to David's city, which is called Bethlehem, because he was of the house and family of David; to enroll himself with Mary, who was pledged to be married to him as wife, being pregnant.

While they were there, the day had come for her to give birth. She gave birth to her firstborn son. She wrapped him in bands of cloth, and laid him in a feeding trough, because there was no room for them in the inn (Luke 2:1-7).

Angels announce birth of Jesus

There were shepherds in the same country staying in the field, and keeping watch by night over their flock. Behold, an angel of the Lord stood by them, and the glory of the Lord shone around them, and they were terrified. The angel said to them, "Don't be afraid, for behold, I bring you good news of great joy which will be to all the people. For there is born to you today, in David's city, a Savior, who is Christ the Lord. This is the sign to you: you will find a baby wrapped in strips of cloth, lying in a feeding trough." Suddenly, there was with the angel a multitude of the heavenly army praising God, and saying,

"Glory to God in the highest,
on earth peace, good will toward men" (Luke 2:8-14).

Shepherds announce birth of Jesus

When the angels went away from them into the sky, the shepherds said to one another, "Let's go to Bethlehem, now, and see this thing that has happened, which the Lord has made known to us." They came with haste, and found both Mary and Joseph, and the baby was lying in the feeding trough. When they saw it, they publicized widely the saying which was spoken to them about this child. All who heard it wondered at the things which were spoken to them by the shepherds. But Mary kept all these sayings, pondering them in her heart. The shepherds returned, glorifying and praising God for all the things that they had heard and seen, just as it was told them (Luke 2:15-20).

Jesus dedicated at Temple at eight days old
When eight days were fulfilled for the circumcision of the child, his name was called Jesus, which was given by the angel before he was conceived in the womb (Luke 2:21).

Mary is ceremonially purified forty days after giving birth
When the days of their purification according to the law of Moses were fulfilled, they brought him up to Jerusalem, to present him to the Lord (as it is written in the law of the Lord, "Every male who opens the womb shall be called holy to the Lord"), and to offer a sacrifice according to that which is said in the law of the Lord, "A pair of turtledoves, or two young pigeons" (Luke 2:22-24).

Prophets foretell Jesus' future
Behold, there was a man in Jerusalem whose name was Simeon. This man was righteous and devout, looking for the consolation of Israel, and the Holy Spirit was on him. It had been revealed to him by the Holy Spirit that he should not see death before he had seen the Lord's Christ. He came in the Spirit into the temple. When the parents brought in the child, Jesus, that they might do concerning him according to the custom of the law, then he received him into his arms, and blessed God, and said,

"Now you are releasing your servant, Master,
 according to your word, in peace;
for my eyes have seen your salvation,
 which you have prepared before the face of all peoples;
a light for revelation to the nations,
 and the glory of your people Israel."

Joseph and his mother were marveling at the things which were spoken concerning him, and Simeon blessed them, and said to Mary, his mother, "Behold, this child is set for the falling and the rising of many in Israel, and for a sign which is spoken against. Yes, a sword will pierce through your own soul, that the thoughts of many hearts may be revealed."

There was one Anna, a prophetess, the daughter of Phanuel, of the tribe of Asher (she was of a great age, having lived with a husband seven years from her virginity, and she had been a widow for about eighty-four years), who didn't depart from the temple, worshiping with fastings and petitions night and day. Coming up at that very hour, she gave thanks to the Lord, and spoke of him to all those who were looking for redemption in Jerusalem (Luke 2:25-38).

Wise men seek, worship Jesus

Now when Jesus was born in Bethlehem of Judea in the days of King Herod, behold, wise men from the east came to Jerusalem, saying, "Where is he who is born King of the Jews? For we saw his star in the east, and have come to worship him." When King Herod heard it, he was troubled, and all Jerusalem with him. Gathering together all the chief priests and scribes of the people, he asked them where the Christ would be born. They said to him, "In Bethlehem of Judea, for this is written through the prophet,

'You Bethlehem, land of Judah,
are in no way least among the princes of Judah:
for out of you shall come a governor,
who shall shepherd my people, Israel.'"

Then Herod secretly called the wise men, and learned from them exactly what time the star appeared. He sent them to Bethlehem, and said, "Go and search diligently for the young child. When you have found him, bring me word, so that I also may come and worship him."

They, having heard the king, went their way; and behold, the star, which they saw in the east, went before them, until it came and stood over where the young child was. When they saw the star, they rejoiced with exceedingly great joy. They came into the house and saw the young child with Mary, his mother, and they fell down and worshiped him. Opening their treasures, they offered to him gifts: gold, frankincense, and myrrh. Being warned in a dream that they shouldn't return to Herod, they went back to their own country another way (Matthew 2:1-12).

Joseph and Mary flee with Jesus to Egypt

Now when they had departed, behold, an angel of the Lord appeared to Joseph in a dream, saying, "Arise and take the young child and his mother, and flee into Egypt, and stay there until I tell you, for Herod will seek the young child to destroy him."

He arose and took the young child and his mother by night, and departed into Egypt, and was there until the death of Herod; that it might be fulfilled which was spoken by the Lord through the prophet, saying, "Out of Egypt I called my son" (Matthew 2:13-15).

Herod orders male children, two years and under, murdered

Then Herod, when he saw that he was mocked by the wise men, was exceedingly angry, and sent out and killed all the male children who were in Bethlehem and in all the surrounding countryside, from two years old and under, according to the exact time which he had learned from the wise men. Then that which was spoken by Jeremiah the prophet was fulfilled, saying,

> "A voice was heard in Ramah,
> lamentation, weeping and great mourning,
> Rachel weeping for her children;
> she wouldn't be comforted,
> because they are no more" (Matthew 2:16-18).

Joseph and Mary take Jesus to Nazareth

But when Herod was dead, behold, an angel of the Lord appeared in a dream to Joseph in Egypt, saying, "Arise and take the young child and his mother, and go into the land of Israel, for those who sought the young child's life are dead."

He arose and took the young child and his mother, and came into the land of Israel. But when he heard that Archelaus was reigning over Judea in the place of his father, Herod, he was afraid to go there. Being warned in a dream, he withdrew into the region of Galilee, and came and lived in a city called Nazareth; that it might be fulfilled which was spoken through the prophets: "He will be called a Nazarene" (Matthew 2:13-23, also Mark 1:24, Luke 2:39, John 1:45).

The childhood of Jesus

The child was growing, and was becoming strong in spirit, being filled with wisdom, and the grace of God was upon him (Luke 2:40).

Jesus impresses religious leaders at twelve years old

His parents went every year to Jerusalem at the feast of the Passover. When he was twelve years old, they went up to Jerusalem according to the custom of the feast, and when they had fulfilled the days, as they were returning, the boy Jesus stayed behind in Jerusalem. Joseph and his mother didn't know it, but supposing him to be in the company, they went a day's journey, and they looked for him among their relatives and acquaintances. When they didn't find him, they returned to Jerusalem, looking for him. After three days they found him in the temple, sitting in the middle of the teachers, both listening to them, and asking them questions. All who heard him were amazed at his understanding and his answers. When they saw him, they were astonished, and his mother said to him, "Son, why have you treated us this way? Behold, your father and I were anxiously looking for you."

He said to them, "Why were you looking for me? Didn't you know that I must be in my Father's house?" They didn't understand the saying which he spoke to them. And he went down with them, and came to Nazareth. He was subject to them, and his mother kept all these sayings in her heart. And Jesus increased in wisdom and stature, and in favor with God and men (Luke 2:41-52).

John the Baptist prepares way for Jesus

Now in the fifteenth year of the reign of Tiberius Caesar, Pontius Pilate being governor of Judea, and Herod being tetrarch of Galilee, and his brother Philip tetrarch of the region of Ituraea and Trachonitis, and Lysanias tetrarch of Abilene, in the high priesthood of Annas and Caiaphas, the word of God came to John, the son of Zacharias, in the wilderness. He came into all the region around the Jordan, preaching the baptism of repentance for remission of sins. As it is written in the book of the words of Isaiah the prophet,

> "The voice of one crying in the wilderness,
> 'Make ready the way of the Lord.
> Make his paths straight.
> Every valley will be filled.
> Every mountain and hill will be brought low.
> The crooked will become straight,
> and the rough ways smooth.
> All flesh will see God's salvation'" (Luke 3:1-6, also
> Matthew 3:1-3, Mark 1:1-8).

Now John himself wore clothing made of camel's hair, with a leather belt around his waist. His food was locusts and wild honey. Then people from Jerusalem, all of Judea, and all the region around the Jordan went out to him. They were baptized by him in the Jordan, confessing their sins. But when he saw many of the Pharisees and Sadducees coming for his baptism, he said to them, "You offspring of vipers, who warned you to flee from the wrath to come? Therefore produce fruit worthy of repentance! Don't think to yourselves, 'We have Abraham for our father,' for I tell you that God is able to raise up children to Abraham from these stones.

"Even now the ax lies at the root of the trees. Therefore every tree that doesn't produce good fruit is cut down, and cast into the fire. I indeed baptize you in water for repentance, but he who comes after me is mightier than I, whose shoes I am not worthy to carry. He will baptize you in the Holy Spirit. His winnowing fork is in his hand, and he will thoroughly cleanse his threshing floor. He will gather his wheat into the barn, but the chaff he will burn up with unquenchable fire" (Matthew 3:4-12).

The multitudes asked him, "What then must we do?"

He answered them, "He who has two coats, let him give to him who has none. He who has food, let him do likewise."

Tax collectors also came to be baptized, and they said to him, "Teacher, what must we do?"

He said to them, "Collect no more than that which is appointed to you."

Soldiers also asked him, saying, "What about us? What must we do?"

He said to them, "Extort from no one by violence, neither accuse anyone wrongfully. Be content with your wages."

As the people were in expectation, and all men reasoned in their hearts concerning John, whether perhaps he was the Christ, John answered them all, "I indeed baptize you with water, but he comes who is mightier than I, the strap of whose sandals I am not worthy to loosen. He will baptize you in the Holy Spirit and fire, whose fan is in his hand, and he will thoroughly cleanse his threshing floor, and will gather the wheat into his barn; but he will burn up the chaff with unquenchable fire."

Then with many other exhortations he preached good news to the people (Luke 3:10-18).

John testified about [Jesus]. He cried out, saying, "This was he of whom I said, 'He who comes after me has surpassed me, for he was before me.'" From his fullness we all received grace upon grace. For the law was given through Moses. Grace and truth were realized through Jesus Christ. No one has seen God at any time. The one and only Son, who is in the bosom of the Father, he has declared him.

This is John's testimony, when the Jews sent priests and Levites from Jerusalem to ask him, "Who are you?"

He declared, and didn't deny, but he declared, "I am not the Christ."

They asked him, "What then? Are you Elijah?"

He said, "I am not."

"Are you the prophet?"

He answered, "No."

They said therefore to him, "Who are you? Give us an answer to take back to those who sent us. What do you say about yourself?"

He said, "I am the voice of one crying in the wilderness, 'Make straight the way of the Lord,' as Isaiah the prophet said."

The ones who had been sent were from the Pharisees. They asked him, "Why then do you baptize, if you are not the Christ, nor Elijah, nor the prophet?"

John answered them, "I baptize in water, but among you stands one whom you don't know. He is the one who comes after me, who is preferred before me, whose sandal strap I'm not worthy to loosen." These things were done in Bethany beyond the Jordan, where John was baptizing (John 1:15-28).

John baptizes Jesus

Then Jesus came from Galilee to the Jordan to John, to be baptized by him. But John would have hindered him, saying, "I need to be baptized by you, and you come to me?"

But Jesus, answering, said to him, "Allow it now, for this is the fitting way for us to fulfill all righteousness." Then he allowed him. Jesus, when he was baptized, went up directly from the water: and behold, the heavens were opened to him. He saw the Spirit of God descending as a dove, and coming on him. Behold, a voice out of the heavens said, "This is my beloved Son, with whom I am well pleased" (Matthew 3:13-17, also Mark 1:9-11, Luke 3:21-22).

Jesus tempted for forty days

Jesus, full of the Holy Spirit, returned from the Jordan, and was led by the Spirit into the wilderness for forty days, being tempted by the devil. He ate nothing in those days. Afterward, when they were completed, he was hungry. The devil said to him, "If you are the Son of God, command this stone to become bread."

Jesus answered him, saying, "It is written, 'Man shall not live by bread alone, but by every word of God.'"

The devil, leading him up on a high mountain, showed him all the kingdoms of the world in a moment of time. The devil said to him, "I will give you all this authority, and their glory, for it has been delivered to me; and I give it to whomever I want. If you therefore will worship before me, it will all be yours."

Jesus answered him, "Get behind me Satan! For it is written, 'You shall worship the Lord your God, and you shall serve him only.'"

He led him to Jerusalem, and set him on the pinnacle of the temple, and said to him, "If you are the Son of God, cast yourself down from here, for it is written,

'He will put his angels in charge of you, to guard you;'
and,
'On their hands they will bear you up,
 lest perhaps you dash your foot against a stone.'"

Jesus answering, said to him, "It has been said, 'You shall not tempt the Lord your God.'"

When the devil had completed every temptation, he departed from him until another time (Luke 4:1-13, also Matthew 4:1-11, Mark 1:12-13).

Jesus begins teaching

Jesus himself, when he began to teach, was about thirty years old (Luke 3:23).

Jesus recruits his first disciples

John was standing with two of his disciples, and he looked at Jesus as he walked, and said, "Behold, the Lamb of God!" The two disciples heard him speak, and they followed Jesus. Jesus turned, and saw them following, and said to them, "What are you looking for?"

They said to him, "Rabbi" (which is to say, being interpreted, Teacher), "where are you staying?"

He said to them, "Come, and see."

They came and saw where he was staying, and they stayed with him that day. It was about the tenth hour. One of the two who heard John, and followed him, was Andrew, Simon Peter's brother. He first found his own brother, Simon, and said to him, "We have found the Messiah!" (which is, being interpreted, Christ). He brought him to Jesus. Jesus looked at him, and said, "You are Simon the son of Jonah. You shall be called Cephas" (which is by interpretation, Peter). On the next day, he was determined to go out into Galilee, and he found Philip. Jesus said to him, "Follow me." Now Philip was from Bethsaida, of the city of Andrew and Peter. Philip found Nathanael, and said to him, "We have found him, of whom Moses in the law, and the prophets, wrote: Jesus of Nazareth, the son of Joseph."

Nathanael said to him, "Can any good thing come out of Nazareth?"

Philip said to him, "Come and see."

Jesus saw Nathanael coming to him, and said about him, "Behold, an Israelite indeed, in whom is no deceit!"

Nathanael said to him, "How do you know me?"

Jesus answered him, "Before Philip called you, when you were under the fig tree, I saw you."

Nathanael answered him, "Rabbi, you are the Son of God! You are King of Israel!"

Jesus answered him, "Because I told you, 'I saw you underneath the fig tree,' do you believe? You will see greater things than these!" He said to him, "Most certainly, I tell you, hereafter you will see heaven opened, and the angels of God ascending and descending on the Son of Man" (John 1:35-51).

Jesus turns water into wine

There was a marriage in Cana of Galilee. Jesus' mother was there. Jesus also was invited, with his disciples, to the marriage. When the wine ran out, Jesus' mother said to him, "They have no wine."

Jesus said to her, "Woman, what does that have to do with you and me? My hour has not yet come."

His mother said to the servants, "Whatever he says to you, do it." Now there were six water pots of stone set there after the Jews' way of purifying, containing [twenty to thirty gallons] apiece. Jesus said to them, "Fill the water pots with water." They filled them up to the brim. He said to them, "Now draw some out, and take it to the ruler of the feast." So they took it. When the ruler of the feast tasted the water now become wine, and didn't know where it came from (but the servants who had drawn the water knew), the ruler of the feast called the bridegroom, and said to him, "Everyone serves the good wine first, and when the guests have drunk freely, then that which is worse. You have kept the good wine until now!" This beginning of his signs Jesus did in Cana of Galilee, and revealed his glory; and his disciples believed in him.

After this, he went down to Capernaum, he, and his mother, his brothers, and his disciples; and they stayed there a few days (John 2:1-12).

Jesus explains being "born anew"

Now there was a man of the Pharisees named Nicodemus, a ruler of the Jews. The same came to him by night, and said to him, "Rabbi, we know that you are a teacher come from God, for no one can do these signs that you do, unless God is with him."

Jesus answered him, "Most certainly, I tell you, unless one is born anew, he can't see God's Kingdom."

Nicodemus said to him, "How can a man be born when he is old? Can he enter a second time into his mother's womb, and be born?"

Jesus answered, "Most certainly I tell you, unless one is born of water and spirit, he can't enter into God's Kingdom! That which is born of the flesh is flesh. That which is born of the Spirit is spirit. Don't marvel that I said to you, 'You must be born anew.' The wind blows where it wants to, and you hear its sound, but don't know where it comes from and where it is going. So is everyone who is born of the Spirit."

Nicodemus answered him, "How can these things be?"

Jesus answered him, "Are you the teacher of Israel, and don't understand these things? Most certainly I tell you, we speak that which we know, and testify of that which we have seen, and you don't receive our witness. If I told you earthly things and you don't believe, how will you believe if I tell you heavenly things? No one has ascended into heaven, but he who descended out of heaven, the Son of Man, who is in heaven. As Moses lifted up the serpent in the wilderness, even so must the Son of Man be lifted up, that whoever believes in him should not perish, but have eternal life. For God so loved the world, that he gave his one and only Son, that whoever believes in him should not perish, but have eternal life. For God didn't send his Son into the world to judge the world, but that the world should be saved through him. He who believes in him is not judged. He who doesn't believe has been judged already, because he has not believed in the name of the one and only Son of God. This is the judgment, that the light has come into the world, and men loved the darkness rather than the light; for their works were evil. For everyone who does evil hates the light, and doesn't come to the light, lest his works would be exposed. But he who does the truth comes to the light, that his works may be revealed, that they have been done in God" (John 3:1-21).

John the Baptist defers attention to Jesus

After these things, Jesus came with his disciples into the land of Judea. He stayed there with them, and baptized. John also was baptizing in Enon near Salim, because there was much water there. They came, and were baptized. For John was not yet thrown into prison. There arose therefore a questioning on the part of John's disciples with some Jews about purification. They came to John, and said to him, "Rabbi, he who was with you beyond the Jordan, to whom you have testified, behold, the same baptizes, and everyone is coming to him."

John answered, "A man can receive nothing, unless it has been given him from heaven. You yourselves testify that I said, 'I am not the Christ,' but, 'I have been sent before him.' He who has the bride is the bridegroom; but the friend of the bridegroom, who stands and hears him, rejoices greatly because of the bridegroom's voice. This, my joy, therefore is made full. He must increase, but I must decrease. He who comes from above is above all. He who is from the earth belongs to the earth, and speaks of the earth. He who comes from heaven is above all. What he has seen and heard, of that he testifies; and no one receives his witness. He who has received his witness has set his seal to this, that God is true. For he whom God has sent speaks the words of God; for God gives the Spirit without measure. The Father loves the Son, and has given all things into his hand. One who believes in the Son has eternal life, but one who disobeys the Son won't see life, but the wrath of God remains on him" (John 3:25-36).

Jesus offers "living water" to Samaritan woman

Therefore when [Jesus] knew that the Pharisees had heard that [he] was making and baptizing more disciples than John (although Jesus himself didn't baptize, but his disciples), he left Judea, and departed into Galilee. He needed to pass through Samaria. So he came to a city of Samaria, called Sychar, near the parcel of ground that Jacob gave to his son, Joseph. Jacob's well was there. Jesus therefore, being tired from his journey, sat down by the well. It was about the sixth hour. A woman of Samaria came to draw water. Jesus said to her, "Give me a drink." For his disciples had gone away into the city to buy food.

The Samaritan woman therefore said to him, "How is it that you, being a Jew, ask for a drink from me, a Samaritan woman?" (For Jews have no dealings with Samaritans.)

Jesus answered her, "If you knew the gift of God, and who it is who says to you, 'Give me a drink,' you would have asked him, and he would have given you living water."

The woman said to him, "Sir, you have nothing to draw with, and the well is deep. So where do you get that living water? Are you greater than our father, Jacob, who gave us the well, and drank of it himself, as did his children, and his livestock?"

Jesus answered her, "Everyone who drinks of this water will thirst again, but whoever drinks of the water that I will give him will never thirst again; but the water that I will give him will become in him a well of water springing up to eternal life."

The woman said to him, "Sir, give me this water, so that I don't get thirsty, neither come all the way here to draw."

Jesus said to her, "Go, call your husband, and come here."

The woman answered, "I have no husband."

Jesus said to her, "You said well, 'I have no husband,' for you have had five husbands; and he whom you now have is not your husband. This you have said truly."

The woman said to him, "Sir, I perceive that you are a prophet. Our fathers worshiped in this mountain, and you Jews say that in Jerusalem is the place where people ought to worship."

Jesus said to her, "Woman, believe me, the hour comes, when neither in this mountain, nor in Jerusalem, will you worship the

Father. You worship that which you don't know. We worship that which we know; for salvation is from the Jews. But the hour comes, and now is, when the true worshipers will worship the Father in spirit and truth, for the Father seeks such to be his worshipers. God is spirit, and those who worship him must worship in spirit and truth."

The woman said to him, "I know that Messiah comes, he who is called Christ. When he has come, he will declare to us all things."

Jesus said to her, "I am he, the one who speaks to you." At this, his disciples came. They marveled that he was speaking with a woman; yet no one said, "What are you looking for?" or, "Why do you speak with her?" So the woman left her water pot, and went away into the city, and said to the people, "Come, see a man who told me everything that I did. Can this be the Christ?" (John 4:1-29).

Jesus explains spiritual food

[The Samaritans] went out of the city, and were coming to him. In the meanwhile, the disciples urged him, saying, "Rabbi, eat."

But he said to them, "I have food to eat that you don't know about."

The disciples therefore said to one another, "Has anyone brought him something to eat?"

Jesus said to them, "My food is to do the will of him who sent me, and to accomplish his work. Don't you say, 'There are yet four months until the harvest?' Behold, I tell you, lift up your eyes, and look at the fields, that they are white for harvest already. He who reaps receives wages, and gathers fruit to eternal life; that both he who sows and he who reaps may rejoice together. For in this the saying is true, 'One sows, and another reaps.' I sent you to reap that for which you haven't labored. Others have labored, and you have entered into their labor" (John 4:30-38).

Many Samaritans believe in Jesus

From that city many of the Samaritans believed in him because of the word of the woman, who testified, "He told me everything that I did." So when the Samaritans came to him, they begged him to stay with them. He stayed there two days. Many more believed because of his word. They said to the woman, "Now we believe, not because of your speaking; for we have heard for ourselves, and know that this is indeed the Christ, the Savior of the world" (John 4:39-42).

Jesus rejected in hometown of Nazareth

Jesus returned in the power of the Spirit into Galilee, and news about him spread through all the surrounding area. He taught in their synagogues, being glorified by all.

He came to Nazareth, where he had been brought up. He entered, as was his custom, into the synagogue on the Sabbath day, and stood up to read. The book of the prophet Isaiah was handed to him. He opened the book, and found the place where it was written,

> "The Spirit of the Lord is on me,
> because he has anointed me to preach good news to the poor.
> He has sent me to heal the broken hearted,
> to proclaim release to the captives,
> recovering of sight to the blind,
> to deliver those who are crushed,
> and to proclaim the acceptable year of the Lord."

He closed the book, gave it back to the attendant, and sat down. The eyes of all in the synagogue were fastened on him. He began to tell them, "Today, this Scripture has been fulfilled in your hearing."

All testified about him, and wondered at the gracious words which proceeded out of his mouth, and they said, "Isn't this Joseph's son?"

He said to them, "Doubtless you will tell me this parable, 'Physician, heal yourself! Whatever we have heard done at Capernaum, do also here in your hometown.'" He said, "Most certainly I tell you, no prophet is acceptable in his hometown. But truly I tell you, there were many widows in Israel in the days of Elijah, when the sky was shut up three years and six months, when a great famine came over all the land. Elijah was sent to none of them, except to Zarephath, in the land of Sidon, to a woman who was a widow. There were many lepers in Israel in the time of Elisha the prophet, yet not one of them was cleansed, except Naaman, the Syrian."

They were all filled with wrath in the synagogue, as they heard these things. They rose up, threw him out of the city, and led him to the brow of the hill that their city was built on, that they might throw him off the cliff. But he, passing through the middle of them, went his way (Luke 4:14-30, also Matthew 13:53-58, Mark 6:1-6).

[Jesus] was in the world, and the world was made through him, and the world didn't recognize him. He came to his own, and those who were his own didn't receive him. But as many as received him, to them he gave the right to become God's children, to those who believe in his name: who were born not of blood, nor of the will of the flesh, nor of the will of man, but of God (John 1:10-13).

Jesus heals nobleman's son

After the two days he went out from there and went into Galilee. For Jesus himself testified that a prophet has no honor in his own country. So when he came into Galilee, the Galileans received him, having seen all the things that he did in Jerusalem at the feast, for they also went to the feast. Jesus came therefore again to Cana of Galilee, where he made the water into wine. There was a certain nobleman whose son was sick at Capernaum. When he heard that Jesus had come out of Judea into Galilee, he went to him, and begged him that he would come down and heal his son, for he was at the point of death. Jesus therefore said to him, "Unless you see signs and wonders, you will in no way believe."

The nobleman said to him, "Sir, come down before my child dies." Jesus said to him, "Go your way. Your son lives." The man believed the word that Jesus spoke to him, and he went his way. As he was now going down, his servants met him and reported, saying "Your child lives!" So he inquired of them the hour when he began to get better. They said therefore to him, "Yesterday at the seventh hour, the fever left him." So the father knew that it was at that hour in which Jesus said to him, "Your son lives." He believed, as did his whole house. This is again the second sign that Jesus did, having come out of Judea into Galilee (John 4:43-54).

Jesus preaches repentance

Leaving Nazareth, he came and lived in Capernaum, which is by the sea, in the region of Zebulun and Naphtali, that it might be fulfilled which was spoken through Isaiah the prophet, saying,

> "The land of Zebulun and the land of Naphtali,
> toward the sea, beyond the Jordan,
> Galilee of the Gentiles,
> the people who sat in darkness saw a great light,
> to those who sat in the region and shadow of death,
> to them light has dawned."

From that time, Jesus began to preach, and to say, "Repent! For the Kingdom of Heaven is at hand" (Matthew 4:13-17, also Mark 1:14-15, Luke 4:14-15).

Jesus recruits additional disciples

Now while the multitude pressed on [Jesus] and heard the word of God, he was standing by the lake of Gennesaret. He saw two boats standing by the lake, but the fishermen had gone out of them, and were washing their nets. He entered into one of the boats, which was Simon's, and asked him to put out a little from the land. He sat down and taught the multitudes from the boat. When he had finished speaking, he said to Simon, "Put out into the deep, and let down your nets for a catch."

Simon answered him, "Master, we worked all night, and took nothing; but at your word I will let down the net." When they had done this, they caught a great multitude of fish, and their net was breaking. They beckoned to their partners in the other boat, that they should come and help them. They came, and filled both boats, so that they began to sink. But Simon Peter, when he saw it, fell down at Jesus' knees, saying, "Depart from me, for I am a sinful man, Lord." For he was amazed, and all who were with him, at the catch of fish which they had caught; and so also were James and John, sons of Zebedee, who were partners with Simon.

Jesus said to Simon, "Don't be afraid. From now on you will be catching people alive."

When they had brought their boats to land, they left everything, and followed him (Luke 5:1-11, also Matthew 4:18-22, Mark 1:16-20).

Jesus heals sick, casts out demons

[Jesus] came down to Capernaum, a city of Galilee. He was teaching them on the Sabbath day, and they were astonished at his teaching, for his word was with authority. In the synagogue there was a man who had a spirit of an unclean demon, and he cried out with a loud voice, saying, "Ah! what have we to do with you, Jesus of Nazareth? Have you come to destroy us? I know you who you are: the Holy One of God!"

Jesus rebuked him, saying, "Be silent, and come out of him!" When the demon had thrown him down in the middle of them, he came out of him, having done him no harm.

Amazement came on all, and they spoke together, one with another, saying, "What is this word? For with authority and power he commands the unclean spirits, and they come out!" News about him went out into every place of the surrounding region.

He rose up from the synagogue, and entered into Simon's house. Simon's mother-in-law was afflicted with a great fever, and they begged him for her. He stood over her, and rebuked the fever; and it left her. Immediately she rose up and served them. When the sun was setting, all those who had any sick with various diseases brought them to him; and he laid his hands on every one of them, and healed them. Demons also came out of many, crying out, and saying, "You are the Christ, the Son of God!" Rebuking them, he didn't allow them to speak, because they knew that he was the Christ (John 4:33-41, also Mark 1:21-34).

Jesus preaches to multitudes

When it was day, [Jesus] departed and went into an uninhabited place, and the multitudes looked for him, and came to him, and held

31

on to him, so that he wouldn't go away from them. But he said to them, "I must preach the good news of God's Kingdom to the other cities also. For this reason I have been sent" (Luke 4:42-43, also Mark 1:35-38).

Jesus went about in all Galilee, teaching in their synagogues, preaching the Good News of the Kingdom, and healing every disease and every sickness among the people. The report about him went out into all Syria. They brought to him all who were sick, afflicted with various diseases and torments, possessed with demons, epileptics, and paralytics; and he healed them. Great multitudes from Galilee, Decapolis, Jerusalem, Judea and from beyond the Jordan followed him (Matthew 4:23-25, also Mark 1:39, John 4:44).

Jesus heals a leper
While he was in one of the cities, behold, there was a man full of leprosy. When he saw Jesus, he fell on his face, and begged him, saying, "Lord, if you want to, you can make me clean."
He stretched out his hand, and touched him, saying, "I want to. Be made clean."
Immediately the leprosy left him. He commanded him to tell no one, "But go your way, and show yourself to the priest, and offer for your cleansing according to what Moses commanded, for a testimony to them." But the report concerning him spread much more, and great multitudes came together to hear, and to be healed by him of their infirmities. But he withdrew himself into the desert, and prayed (Luke 5:12-16, also Matthew 8:1-4, Mark 1:40-45).

Jesus heals a paralyzed man
On one of those days, he was teaching; and there were Pharisees and teachers of the law sitting by, who had come out of every village of Galilee, Judea, and Jerusalem. The power of the Lord was with him to heal them. Behold, men brought a paralyzed man on a cot, and they sought to bring him in to lay before Jesus. Not finding a way to bring him in because of the multitude, they went up to the housetop, and let him down through the tiles with his cot into the middle before Jesus. Seeing their faith, he said to him, "Man, your

sins are forgiven you" (Luke 5:17-20, also Matthew 9:1-8, Mark 2:1-12).

Religious leaders challenge Jesus

The scribes and the Pharisees began to reason, saying, "Who is this that speaks blasphemies? Who can forgive sins, but God alone?"

But Jesus, perceiving their thoughts, answered them, "Why are you reasoning so in your hearts? Which is easier to say, 'Your sins are forgiven you;' or to say, 'Arise and walk?' But that you may know that the Son of Man has authority on earth to forgive sins" (he said to the paralyzed man), "I tell you, arise, and take up your cot, and go to your house."

Immediately he rose up before them, and took up that which he was laying on, and departed to his house, glorifying God. Amazement took hold on all, and they glorified God. They were filled with fear, saying, "We have seen strange things today" (Luke 5:21-26, also Matthew 9:2-8, Mark 2:1-12).

Jesus recruits Levi, the tax collector, as disciple

After these things [Jesus] went out, and saw a tax collector named Levi sitting at the tax office, and said to him, "Follow me!"

[Levi] left everything, and rose up and followed him. Levi made a great feast for him in his house. There was a great crowd of tax collectors and others who were reclining with them. Their scribes and the Pharisees murmured against his disciples, saying, "Why do you eat and drink with the tax collectors and sinners?" Jesus answered them, "Those who are healthy have no need for a physician, but those who are sick do. I have not come to call the righteous, but sinners to repentance."

They said to him, "Why do John's disciples often fast and pray, likewise also the disciples of the Pharisees, but yours eat and drink?"

He said to them, "Can you make the friends of the bridegroom fast, while the bridegroom is with them? But the days will come when the bridegroom will be taken away from them. Then they will fast in those days" (Luke 5:27-35, also Matthew 9:9-17, Mark 2:13-22).

Jesus heals paralyzed man

After these things, there was a feast of the Jews, and Jesus went up to Jerusalem. Now in Jerusalem by the sheep gate, there is a pool, which is called in Hebrew, "Bethesda", having five porches. In these lay a great multitude of those who were sick, blind, lame, or paralyzed, waiting for the moving of the water; for an angel went down at certain times into the pool, and stirred up the water. Whoever stepped in first after the stirring of the water was healed of whatever disease he had. A certain man was there, who had been sick for thirty-eight years. When Jesus saw him lying there, and knew that he had been sick for a long time, he asked him, "Do you want to be made well?"

The sick man answered him, "Sir, I have no one to put me into the pool when the water is stirred up, but while I'm coming, another steps down before me."

Jesus said to him, "Arise, take up your mat, and walk."

Immediately, the man was made well, and took up his mat and walked (John 5:1-9a).

Jesus challenged for healing on the Jewish Sabbath

Now it was the Sabbath on that day. So the Jews said to him who was cured, "It is the Sabbath. It is not lawful for you to carry the mat."

He answered them, "He who made me well, the same said to me, 'Take up your mat, and walk.'"

Then they asked him, "Who is the man who said to you, 'Take up your mat, and walk'?"

But he who was healed didn't know who it was, for Jesus had withdrawn, a crowd being in the place.

Afterward Jesus found him in the temple, and said to him, "Behold, you are made well. Sin no more, so that nothing worse happens to you."

The man went away, and told the Jews that it was Jesus who had made him well. For this cause the Jews persecuted Jesus, and sought to kill him, because he did these things on the Sabbath (John 5:9b-16).

[See Lessons: **Jesus teaches about himself** (John 9:17-47).]

34

Jesus angers religious leaders over Sabbath laws

At that time, Jesus went on the Sabbath day through the grain fields. His disciples were hungry and began to pluck heads of grain and to eat. But the Pharisees, when they saw it, said to him, "Behold, your disciples do what is not lawful to do on the Sabbath."

But he said to them, "Haven't you read what David did, when he was hungry, and those who were with him; how he entered into God's house, and ate the show bread, which was not lawful for him to eat, neither for those who were with him, but only for the priests? Or have you not read in the law, that on the Sabbath day, the priests in the temple profane the Sabbath, and are guiltless? But I tell you that one greater than the temple is here. But if you had known what this means, 'I desire mercy, and not sacrifice,' you would not have condemned the guiltless. For the Son of Man is Lord of the Sabbath" (Matthew 12:1-8, also Mark 2:23-28, Luke 6:1-5).

It also happened on another Sabbath that he entered into the synagogue and taught. There was a man there, and his right hand was withered. The scribes and the Pharisees watched him, to see whether he would heal on the Sabbath, that they might find an accusation against him. But he knew their thoughts; and he said to the man who had the withered hand, "Rise up, and stand in the middle." He arose and stood. Then Jesus said to them, "I will ask you something: Is it lawful on the Sabbath to do good, or to do harm? To save a life, or to kill?" He looked around at them all, and said to the man, "Stretch out your hand." He did, and his hand was restored as sound as the other. But they were filled with rage, and talked with one another about what they might do to Jesus (Luke 6:6-11, also Matthew 12:9-14, Mark 3:1-6).

But the Pharisees went out, and conspired against him, how they might destroy him. Jesus, perceiving that, withdrew from there. Great multitudes followed him; and he healed them all, and commanded them that they should not make him known: that it might be fulfilled which was spoken through Isaiah the prophet, saying,

"Behold, my servant whom I have chosen;
my beloved in whom my soul is well pleased:
I will put my Spirit on him.
He will proclaim justice to the nations.
He will not strive, nor shout;
neither will anyone hear his voice in the streets.
He won't break a bruised reed.
He won't quench a smoking flax,
until he leads justice to victory.
In his name, the nations will hope" (Matthew 12:14-21).

Many people follow Jesus to be healed

Jesus withdrew to the sea with his disciples, and a great multitude followed him from Galilee, from Judea, from Jerusalem, from Idumaea, beyond the Jordan, and those from around Tyre and Sidon. A great multitude, hearing what great things he did, came to him. He spoke to his disciples that a little boat should stay near him because of the crowd, so that they wouldn't press on him. For he had healed many, so that as many as had diseases pressed on him that they might touch him. The unclean spirits, whenever they saw him, fell down before him, and cried, "You are the Son of God!" He sternly warned them that they should not make him known (Mark 3:7-12, also Matthew 4:23-25).

Jesus chooses twelve apostles

In these days, [Jesus] went out to the mountain to pray, and he continued all night in prayer to God. When it was day, he called his disciples, and from them he chose twelve, whom he also named apostles: Simon, whom he also named Peter; Andrew, his brother; James; John; Philip; Bartholomew; Matthew; Thomas; James, the son of Alphaeus; Simon, who was called the Zealot; Judas the son of James; and Judas Iscariot, who also became a traitor (Luke 6:12-16, also Matthew 10:1-4, Mark 3:13-19).

Jesus teaches on level place

He came down with them, and stood on a level place, with a crowd of his disciples, and a great number of the people from all Judea and Jerusalem, and the sea coast of Tyre and Sidon, who came to hear him and to be healed of their diseases; as well as those who were troubled by unclean spirits, and they were being healed. All the multitude sought to touch him, for power came out of him and healed them all.

He lifted up his eyes to his disciples, and he taught them] (Luke 6:17-20).

[See Lessons: **Blessings, False prophets, Forgiveness, Love, Judgment** (Luke 6:20-49).]

Jesus teaches on mountain

Seeing the multitudes, he went up onto the mountain. When he had sat down, his disciples came to him. He opened his mouth and taught them (Matthew 5:1-2).

[See Lessons: **Anger, Anxiety, Blessings, Divorce, False Prophets Fasting, Forgiveness, Generosity, Humility, Judgment, the Law, Love, Lust, Persecution, Prayer, Reconciliation, Temptation, Treasures, Vows, Witnessing** (Matthew 5:1-7:29).]

Jesus heals a centurion's son

After he had finished speaking in the hearing of the people, he entered into Capernaum. A certain centurion's servant, who was dear to him, was sick and at the point of death. When he heard about Jesus, he sent to him elders of the Jews, asking him to come and save his servant. When they came to Jesus, they begged him earnestly, saying, "He is worthy for you to do this for him, for he loves our nation, and he built our synagogue for us." Jesus went with them. When he was now not far from the house, the centurion sent friends to him, saying to him, "Lord, don't trouble yourself, for I am not worthy for you to come under my roof. Therefore I didn't even think myself worthy to come to you; but say the word, and my servant will be healed. For I also am a man placed under authority, having under myself soldiers. I tell this one, 'Go!' and he goes; and to another, 'Come!' and he comes; and to my servant, 'Do this,' and he does it."

When Jesus heard these things, he marveled at him, and turned and said to the multitude who followed him, "I tell you, I have not found such great faith, no, not in Israel." Those who were sent, returning to the house, found that the servant who had been sick was well (Luke 7:1-10, also Matthew 8:5-13, John 4:46-54).

Jesus raises widow's son from dead

Soon afterwards, he went to a city called Nain. Many of his disciples, along with a great multitude, went with him. Now when he came near to the gate of the city, behold, one who was dead was carried out, the only son of his mother, and she was a widow. Many people of the city were with her. When the Lord saw her, he had compassion on her, and said to her, "Don't cry." He came near and touched the coffin, and the bearers stood still. He said, "Young man, I tell you, arise!" He who was dead sat up, and began to speak. And he gave him to his mother.

Fear took hold of all, and they glorified God, saying, "A great prophet has arisen among us!" and, "God has visited his people!" This report went out concerning him in the whole of Judea, and in all the surrounding region (Luke 7:11-17).

Jesus commends John the Baptist

The disciples of John told him about all these things. John, calling to himself two of his disciples, sent them to Jesus, saying, "Are you the one who is coming, or should we look for another?" When the men had come to him, they said, "John the Baptizer has sent us to you, saying, 'Are you he who comes, or should we look for another?'"

In that hour [Jesus] healed many of diseases and plagues and evil spirits; and to many who were blind he gave sight. Jesus answered them, "Go and tell John the things which you have seen and heard: that the blind receive their sight, the lame walk, the lepers are cleansed, the deaf hear, the dead are raised up, and the poor have good news preached to them. Blessed is he who finds no occasion for stumbling in me."

When John's messengers had departed, he began to tell the multitudes about John, "What did you go out into the wilderness to see? A reed shaken by the wind? But what did you go out to see? A man clothed in soft clothing? Behold, those who are gorgeously dressed, and live delicately, are in kings' courts. But what did you go out to see? A prophet? Yes, I tell you, and much more than a prophet. This is he of whom it is written,

'Behold, I send my messenger before your face,
   who will prepare your way before you.'

"For I tell you, among those who are born of women there is not a greater prophet than John the Baptizer, yet he who is least in God's Kingdom is greater than he."

When all the people and the tax collectors heard this, they declared God to be just, having been baptized with John's baptism. But the Pharisees and the lawyers rejected the counsel of God, not being baptized by him themselves.

"To what then will I liken the people of this generation? What are they like? They are like children who sit in the marketplace, and call to one another, saying, 'We piped to you, and you didn't dance. We mourned, and you didn't weep.' For John the Baptizer came neither eating bread nor drinking wine, and you say, 'He has a demon.' The Son of Man has come eating and drinking, and you say, 'Behold, a gluttonous man, and a drunkard; a friend of tax collectors and sinners!' Wisdom is justified by all her children" (Luke 7:18-35, also Matthew 11:2-19).

Jesus denounces unrepentant cities

Then he began to denounce the cities in which most of his mighty works had been done, because they didn't repent. "Woe to you, Chorazin! Woe to you, Bethsaida! For if the mighty works had been done in Tyre and Sidon which were done in you, they would have repented long ago in sackcloth and ashes. But I tell you, it will be more tolerable for Tyre and Sidon on the day of judgment than for you. You, Capernaum, who are exalted to heaven, you will go down to Hades. For if the mighty works had been done in Sodom which were done in you, it would have remained until today. But I tell you that it will be more tolerable for the land of Sodom, on the day of judgment, than for you" (Matthew 11:20-24 also Luke 10:13-15).

Jesus dines with Pharisee, anointed by "sinner"

One of the Pharisees invited him to eat with him. He entered into the Pharisee's house, and sat at the table. Behold, a woman in the city who was a sinner, when she knew that he was reclining in the Pharisee's house, she brought an alabaster jar of ointment. Standing behind at his feet weeping, she began to wet his feet with her tears, and she wiped them with the hair of her head, kissed his feet, and anointed them with the ointment. Now when the Pharisee who had invited him saw it, he said to himself, "This man, if he were a prophet, would have perceived who and what kind of woman this is who touches him, that she is a sinner."

Jesus answered him, "Simon, I have something to tell you."

He said, "Teacher, say on."

"A certain lender had two debtors. The one owed five hundred [day's wages] and the other fifty. When they couldn't pay, he forgave them both. Which of them therefore will love him most?"

Simon answered, "He, I suppose, to whom he forgave the most."

He said to him, "You have judged correctly." Turning to the woman, he said to Simon, "Do you see this woman? I entered into your house, and you gave me no water for my feet, but she has wet my feet with her tears, and wiped them with the hair of her head. You gave me no kiss, but she, since the time I came in, has not ceased to kiss my feet. You didn't anoint my head with oil, but she has anointed my feet with ointment. Therefore I tell you, her sins, which are many, are forgiven, for she loved much. But to whom little is forgiven, the same loves little." He said to her, "Your sins are forgiven."

Those who sat at the table with him began to say to themselves, "Who is this who even forgives sins?"

He said to the woman, "Your faith has saved you. Go in peace" (Luke 7:36-50).

Jesus includes women among followers

Soon afterwards, he went about through cities and villages, preaching and bringing the good news of God's Kingdom. With him were the twelve, and certain women who had been healed of evil spirits and infirmities: Mary who was called Magdalene, from whom seven demons had gone out; and Joanna, the wife of Chuzas, Herod's steward; Susanna; and many others; who served them from their possessions (Luke 8:1-3).

Jesus accused of casting out demons by the power of Satan

Then one possessed by a demon, blind and mute, was brought to [Jesus] and he healed him, so that the blind and mute man both spoke and saw. All the multitudes were amazed, and said, "Can this be the son of David?" But when the Pharisees heard it, they said, "This man does not cast out demons, except by Beelzebul, the prince of the demons."

Knowing their thoughts, Jesus said to them, "Every kingdom divided against itself is brought to desolation, and every city or house divided against itself will not stand. If Satan casts out Satan, he is divided against himself. How then will his kingdom stand? If I by Beelzebul cast out demons, by whom do your children cast them out? Therefore they will be your judges. But if I by the Spirit of God cast out demons, then God's Kingdom has come upon you. Or how can one enter into the house of the strong man, and plunder his goods, unless he first bind the strong man? Then he will plunder his house.

"He who is not with me is against me, and he who doesn't gather with me, scatters. Therefore I tell you, every sin and blasphemy will be forgiven men, but the blasphemy against the Spirit will not be forgiven men. Whoever speaks a word against the Son of Man, it will be forgiven him; but whoever speaks against the Holy Spirit, it will not be forgiven him, neither in this age, nor in that which is to come (Matthew 12:22-32, also Mark 3:20-30, Luke 11:14-23).

Pharisees demand proof of Jesus' authority

Then certain of the scribes and Pharisees answered, "Teacher, we want to see a sign from you."

But he answered them, "An evil and adulterous generation seeks after a sign, but no sign will be given it but the sign of Jonah the prophet. For as Jonah was three days and three nights in the belly of the whale, so will the Son of Man be three days and three nights in the heart of the earth. The men of Nineveh will stand up in the judgment with this generation, and will condemn it, for they repented at the preaching of Jonah; and behold, someone greater than Jonah is here. The queen of the south will rise up in the judgment with this generation, and will condemn it, for she came from the ends of the earth to hear the wisdom of Solomon; and behold, someone greater than Solomon is here.

When an unclean spirit has gone out of a man, he passes through waterless places, seeking rest, and doesn't find it. Then he says, 'I will return into my house from which I came out,' and when he has come back, he finds it empty, swept, and put in order. Then he goes, and takes with himself seven other spirits more evil than he is, and they enter in and dwell there. The last state of that man becomes worse than the first. Even so will it be also to this evil generation" (Matthew 12:38-45, Luke 11:29-32).

Jesus includes all believers in his family

While he was yet speaking to the multitudes, behold, his mother and his brothers stood outside, seeking to speak to him. One said to him, "Behold, your mother and your brothers stand outside, seeking to speak to you."

But he answered him who spoke to him, "Who is my mother? Who are my brothers?" He stretched out his hand towards his disciples, and said, "Behold, my mother and my brothers! For whoever does the will of my Father who is in heaven, he is my brother, and sister, and mother" (Matthew 12:46-50, also Mark 3:31-35, Luke 8:19-21).

Jesus calms a storm at sea

On that day, when evening had come, he said to them, "Let's go over to the other side." Leaving the multitude, they took him with them, even as he was, in the boat. Other small boats were also with him. A big wind storm arose, and the waves beat into the boat, so much that the boat was already filled. He himself was in the stern, asleep on the cushion, and they woke him up, and told him, "Teacher, don't you care that we are dying?"

He awoke, and rebuked the wind, and said to the sea, "Peace! Be still!" The wind ceased, and there was a great calm. He said to them, "Why are you so afraid? How is it that you have no faith?"

They were greatly afraid, and said to one another, "Who then is this, that even the wind and the sea obey him?" (Mark 4:35-41, also Matthew 8:23-27, Luke 8:22-25).

Jesus casts out demons

They came to the other side of the sea, into the country of the Gadarenes. When he had come out of the boat, immediately a man with an unclean spirit met him out of the tombs. He lived in the tombs. Nobody could bind him any more, not even with chains, because he had been often bound with fetters and chains, and the chains had been torn apart by him, and the fetters broken in pieces. Nobody had the strength to tame him. Always, night and day, in the tombs and in the mountains, he was crying out, and cutting himself with stones. When he saw Jesus from afar, he ran and bowed down to him, and crying out with a loud voice, he said, "What have I to do with you, Jesus, you Son of the Most High God? I adjure you by God, don't torment me." For he said to him, "Come out of the man, you unclean spirit!"

He asked him, "What is your name?"

He said to him, "My name is Legion, for we are many." He begged him much that he would not send them away out of the country. Now on the mountainside there was a great herd of pigs feeding. All the demons begged him, saying, "Send us into the pigs, that we may enter into them."

At once Jesus gave them permission. The unclean spirits came out and entered into the pigs. The herd of about two thousand rushed down the steep bank into the sea, and they were drowned in the sea. Those who fed them fled, and told it in the city and in the country.

The people came to see what it was that had happened. They came to Jesus, and saw him who had been possessed by demons sitting, clothed, and in his right mind, even him who had the legion;

and they were afraid. Those who saw it declared to them what happened to him who was possessed by demons, and about the pigs. They began to beg him to depart from their region.

As he was entering into the boat, he who had been possessed by demons begged him that he might be with him. He didn't allow him, but said to him, "Go to your house, to your friends, and tell them what great things the Lord has done for you, and how he had mercy on you."

He went his way, and began to proclaim in Decapolis how Jesus had done great things for him, and everyone marveled (Mark 5:1-20, also Matthew 8:28-34, Luke 8:26-39).

Jesus heals daughter of synagogue ruler, woman

When Jesus had crossed back over in the boat to the other side, a great multitude was gathered to him; and he was by the sea. Behold, one of the rulers of the synagogue, Jairus by name, came; and seeing him, he fell at his feet, and begged him much, saying, "My little daughter is at the point of death. Please come and lay your hands on her, that she may be made healthy, and live."

He went with him, and a great multitude followed him, and they pressed upon him on all sides. A certain woman, who had an issue of blood for twelve years, and had suffered many things by many physicians, and had spent all that she had, and was no better, but rather grew worse, having heard the things concerning Jesus, came up behind him in the crowd, and touched his clothes. For she said, "If I just touch his clothes, I will be made well." Immediately the flow of her blood was dried up, and she felt in her body that she was healed of her affliction.

Immediately Jesus, perceiving in himself that the power had gone out from him, turned around in the crowd, and asked, "Who touched my clothes?"

His disciples said to him, "You see the multitude pressing against you, and you say, 'Who touched me?'"

He looked around to see her who had done this thing. But the woman, fearing and trembling, knowing what had been done to her, came and fell down before him, and told him all the truth.

He said to her, "Daughter, your faith has made you well. Go in peace, and be cured of your disease."

While he was still speaking, people came from the synagogue ruler's house saying, "Your daughter is dead. Why bother the Teacher any more?"

But Jesus, when he heard the message spoken, immediately said to the ruler of the synagogue, "Don't be afraid, only believe." He allowed no one to follow him, except Peter, James, and John the brother of James. He came to the synagogue ruler's house, and he saw an uproar, weeping, and great wailing. When he had entered in, he said to them, "Why do you make an uproar and weep? The child is not dead, but is asleep."

They ridiculed him. But he, having put them all out, took the father of the child, her mother, and those who were with him, and went in where the child was lying. Taking the child by the hand, he said to her, "*Talitha cumi*!" which means, being interpreted, "Girl, I tell you, get up!" Immediately the girl rose up and walked, for she was twelve years old. They were amazed with great amazement. He strictly ordered them that no one should know this, and commanded that something should be given to her to eat (Mark 5:21-43, also Matthew 9:18-26, Luke 8:40-56).

Jesus heals two blind men

As Jesus passed by from there, two blind men followed him, calling out and saying, "Have mercy on us, son of David!"

When he had come into the house, the blind men came to him. Jesus said to them, "Do you believe that I am able to do this?"

They told him, "Yes, Lord."

Then he touched their eyes, saying, "According to your faith be it done to you." Their eyes were opened. Jesus strictly commanded them, saying, "See that no one knows about this." But they went out and spread abroad his fame in all that land (Matthew 9:27-31).

Jesus heals a mute man

As they went out, behold, a mute man who was demon possessed was brought to him. When the demon was cast out, the mute man spoke. The multitudes marveled, saying, "Nothing like this has ever been seen in Israel!"

But the Pharisees said, "By the prince of the demons, he casts out demons" (Matthew 9:32-34).

Jesus once again rejected

He went out from there. He came into his own country, and his disciples followed him. When the Sabbath had come, he began to teach in the synagogue, and many hearing him were astonished, saying, "Where did this man get these things?" and, "What is the wisdom that is given to this man, that such mighty works come about by his hands? Isn't this the carpenter, the son of Mary, and brother of James, Joses, Judah, and Simon? Aren't his sisters here with us?" They were offended at him.

Jesus said to them, "A prophet is not without honor, except in his own country, and among his own relatives, and in his own house." He could do no mighty work there, except that he laid his hands on a few sick people, and healed them. He marveled because of their unbelief (Mark 6:1-6, also Matthew 13:54-58).

Jesus sends out his disciples

Jesus went about all the cities and the villages, teaching in their synagogues, and preaching the Good News of the Kingdom, and healing every disease and every sickness among the people. But when he saw the multitudes, he was moved with compassion for them, because they were harassed and scattered, like sheep without a shepherd. Then he said to his disciples, "The harvest indeed is plentiful, but the laborers are few. Pray therefore that the Lord of the harvest will send out laborers into his harvest."

He called to himself his twelve disciples, and gave them authority over unclean spirits, to cast them out, and to heal every disease and every sickness.

Jesus sent these twelve out, and commanded them, saying, "Don't go among the Gentiles, and don't enter into any city of the Samaritans. Rather, go to the lost sheep of the house of Israel. As you go, preach, saying, 'The Kingdom of Heaven is at hand!' Heal the sick, cleanse the lepers, and cast out demons. Freely you received, so freely give. Don't take any gold, silver, or brass in your money belts. Take no bag for your journey, neither two coats, nor shoes, nor staff: for the laborer is worthy of his food. Into whatever city or village you enter, find out who in it is worthy; and stay there until you go on. As you enter into the household, greet it. If the household is worthy, let your peace come on it, but if it isn't worthy, let your peace return to you. Whoever doesn't receive you, nor hear your words, as you go out of that house or that city, shake off the dust from your feet. Most certainly I tell you, it will be more tolerable for the land of Sodom and Gomorrah in the day of judgment than for that city.

"Behold, I send you out as sheep among wolves. Therefore be wise as serpents, and harmless as doves (Matthew 9:35-10:1, 5-16, also Mark 6:7-13, Luke 9:1-6).

Jesus warns about persecution
[See Lessons: **Persecution** (Matthew 10:16-11:1)]

John the Baptist executed
[The disciples] went out and preached that people should repent. They cast out many demons, and anointed many with oil who were sick, and healed them. King Herod heard this, for [Jesus'] name had become known, and he said, "John the Baptizer has risen from the dead, and therefore these powers are at work in him." But others said, "He is Elijah." Others said, "He is a prophet, or like one of the prophets." But Herod, when he heard this, said, "This is John, whom I beheaded. He has risen from the dead." For Herod himself had sent out and arrested John, and bound him in prison for the sake of Herodias, his brother Philip's wife, for he had married her. For John said to Herod, "It is not lawful for you to have your brother's wife." Herodias set herself against him, and desired to kill him, but she couldn't, for Herod feared John, knowing that he was a righteous and holy man, and kept him safe. When he heard him, he did many things, and he heard him gladly.

Then a convenient day came, that Herod on his birthday made a supper for his nobles, the high officers, and the chief men of Galilee. When the daughter of Herodias herself came in and danced, she pleased Herod and those sitting with him. The king said to the young lady, "Ask me whatever you want, and I will give it to you." He swore to her, "Whatever you shall ask of me, I will give you, up to half of my kingdom."

She went out, and said to her mother, "What shall I ask?"

She said, "The head of John the Baptizer."

She came in immediately with haste to the king, and asked, "I want you to give me right now the head of John the Baptizer on a platter."

The king was exceedingly sorry, but for the sake of his oaths, and of his dinner guests, he didn't wish to refuse her. Immediately the king sent out a soldier of his guard, and commanded to bring John's head, and he went and beheaded him in the prison, and brought his head on a platter, and gave it to the young lady; and the young lady gave it to her mother.

When his disciples heard this, they came and took up his corpse, and laid it in a tomb (Mark 6:14-29, also Matthew 14:1-12, Luke 9:7-9).

Jesus feeds multitude with five loaves and two fish

The apostles gathered themselves together to Jesus, and they told him all things, whatever they had done, and whatever they had taught. He said to them, "You come apart into a deserted place, and rest awhile." For there were many coming and going, and they had no leisure so much as to eat. They went away in the boat to a deserted place by themselves. They saw them going, and many recognized him and ran there on foot from all the cities. They arrived before them and came together to him. Jesus came out, saw a great multitude, and he had compassion on them, because they were like sheep without a shepherd, and he began to teach them many things. When it was late in the day, his disciples came to him, and said, "This place is deserted, and it is late in the day. Send them away, that they may go into the surrounding country and villages, and buy themselves bread, for they have nothing to eat."

But he answered them, "You give them something to eat."

They asked him, "Shall we go and buy [a year's wages] worth of bread, and give them something to eat?"

He said to them, "How many loaves do you have? Go see."

When they knew, they said, "Five, and two fish."

He commanded them that everyone should sit down in groups on the green grass. They sat down in ranks, by hundreds and by fifties. He took the five loaves and the two fish, and looking up to heaven, he blessed and broke the loaves, and he gave to his disciples to set before them, and he divided the two fish among them all. They all ate, and were filled. They took up twelve baskets full of broken pieces and also of the fish. Those who ate the loaves were five thousand men (Mark 6:30-44, also Matthew 14:13-21, Luke 9:9:10-17, John 6:1-13).

Jesus flees when crowd wants to make him king

When therefore the people saw the sign which Jesus did, they said, "This is truly the prophet who comes into the world." Jesus therefore, perceiving that they were about to come and take him by force, to make him king, withdrew again to the mountain by himself.

When evening came, his disciples went down to the sea, and they entered into the boat, and were going over the sea to Capernaum. It was now dark, and Jesus had not come to them (John 6:14-17).

Jesus walks on water, calms storm

But the boat was now in the middle of the sea, distressed by the waves, for the wind was contrary. In the fourth watch of the night, Jesus came to them, walking on the sea. When the disciples saw him walking on the sea, they were troubled, saying, "It's a ghost!" and they cried out for fear. But immediately Jesus spoke to them, saying "Cheer up! It is I! Don't be afraid."

Peter answered him and said, "Lord, if it is you, command me to come to you on the waters."

He said, "Come!"

Peter stepped down from the boat, and walked on the waters to come to Jesus. But when he saw that the wind was strong, he was afraid, and beginning to sink, he cried out, saying, "Lord, save me!"

Immediately Jesus stretched out his hand, took hold of him, and said to him, "You of little faith, why did you doubt?" When they got up into the boat, the wind ceased. Those who were in the boat came and worshiped him, saying, "You are truly the Son of God!"

When they had crossed over, they came to the land of Gennesaret. When the people of that place recognized him, they sent into all that surrounding region, and brought to him all who were sick, and they begged him that they might just touch the fringe of his garment. As many as touched it were made whole (Matthew 14:24-36, Mark 6:35-52, John 6:15-21).

Jesus confronts religious leaders' hypocrisy

Then Pharisees and scribes came to Jesus from Jerusalem, saying, "Why do your disciples disobey the tradition of the elders? For they don't wash their hands when they eat bread."

He answered them, "Why do you also disobey the commandment of God because of your tradition?" (Matthew 15:1-3).

[See Lessons: **Hypocrisy** (Matthew 15:2-20, also Mark 7:1-16).]

Jesus casts out girl's demon

Jesus went out from there, and withdrew into the region of Tyre and Sidon. Behold, a Canaanite woman came out from those borders, and cried, saying, "Have mercy on me, Lord, you son of David! My daughter is severely possessed by a demon!"

But he answered her not a word.

His disciples came and begged him, saying, "Send her away; for she cries after us."

But he answered, "I wasn't sent to anyone but the lost sheep of the house of Israel."

But she came and worshiped him, saying, "Lord, help me."

But he answered, "It is not appropriate to take the children's bread and throw it to the dogs."

But she said, "Yes, Lord, but even the dogs eat the crumbs which fall from their masters' table."

Then Jesus answered her, "Woman, great is your faith! Be it done to you even as you desire." And her daughter was healed from that hour (Matthew 15:21-28, also Mark 7:24-30).

Jesus heals deaf man

Again [Jesus] departed from the borders of Tyre and Sidon, and came to the sea of Galilee, through the middle of the region of

Decapolis. They brought to him one who was deaf and had an impediment in his speech. They begged him to lay his hand on him. He took him aside from the multitude, privately, and put his fingers into his ears, and he spat, and touched his tongue. Looking up to heaven, he sighed, and said to him, *"Ephphatha!"* that is, "Be opened!" Immediately his ears were opened, and the impediment of his tongue was released, and he spoke clearly. He commanded them that they should tell no one, but the more he commanded them, so much the more widely they proclaimed it. They were astonished beyond measure, saying, "He has done all things well. He makes even the deaf hear, and the mute speak!" (Mark 7:31-37).

Jesus, heals and feeds multitude

Jesus departed there, and came near to the sea of Galilee; and he went up into the mountain, and sat there. Great multitudes came to him, having with them the lame, blind, mute, maimed, and many others, and they put them down at his feet. He healed them, so that the multitude wondered when they saw the mute speaking, injured whole, lame walking, and blind seeing—and they glorified the God of Israel.

Jesus summoned his disciples and said, "I have compassion on the multitude, because they continue with me now three days and have nothing to eat. I don't want to send them away fasting, or they might faint on the way."

The disciples said to him, "Where should we get so many loaves in a deserted place as to satisfy so great a multitude?"

Jesus said to them, "How many loaves do you have?"

They said, "Seven, and a few small fish."

He commanded the multitude to sit down on the ground; and he took the seven loaves and the fish. He gave thanks and broke them, and gave to the disciples, and the disciples to the multitudes. They all ate, and were filled. They took up seven baskets full of the broken pieces that were left over. Those who ate were four thousand men, besides women and children. Then he sent away the multitudes, got into the boat, and came into the borders of Magdala (Matthew 15:29-35, also Mark 8:1-10).

Jesus again asked for sign of his authority

The Pharisees and Sadducees came, and testing him, asked him to show them a sign from heaven. But he answered them, "When it is evening, you say, 'It will be fair weather, for the sky is red.' In the morning, 'It will be foul weather today, for the sky is red and threatening.' Hypocrites! You know how to discern the appearance of the sky, but you can't discern the signs of the times! An evil and adulterous generation seeks after a sign, and there will be no sign given to it, except the sign of the prophet Jonah."

He left them, and departed (Matthew 16:1-4, also Mark 8:11-13, Luke 12:54-56).

Jesus warns disciples concerning religious leaders

The disciples came to the other side and had forgotten to take bread. Jesus said to them, "Take heed and beware of the yeast of the Pharisees and Sadducees."

They reasoned among themselves, saying, "We brought no bread."

Jesus, perceiving it, said, "Why do you reason among yourselves, you of little faith, 'because you have brought no bread?' Don't you yet perceive, neither remember the five loaves for the five thousand, and how many baskets you took up? Nor the seven loaves for the four thousand, and how many baskets you took up? How is it that you don't perceive that I didn't speak to you concerning bread? But beware of the yeast of the Pharisees and Sadducees."

Then they understood that he didn't tell them to beware of the yeast of bread, but of the teaching of the Pharisees and Sadducees (Matthew 16:5-12, also Mark 8:13-21).

Jesus heals blind man

He came to Bethsaida. They brought a blind man to him, and begged him to touch him. He took hold of the blind man by the hand, and brought him out of the village. When he had spit on his eyes, and laid his hands on him, he asked him if he saw anything.

He looked up, and said, "I see men; for I see them like trees walking."

Then again he laid his hands on his eyes. He looked intently, and was restored, and saw everyone clearly. He sent him away to his house, saying, "Don't enter into the village, nor tell anyone in the village" (Mark 8:22-26).

Peter recognizes Jesus is the Christ

Jesus went out, with his disciples, into the villages of Caesarea Philippi. On the way he asked his disciples, "Who do men say that I am?"

They told him, "John the Baptizer, and others say Elijah, but others: one of the prophets."

He said to them, "But who do you say that I am?"

Peter answered, "You are the Christ."

He commanded them that they should tell no one about him (Mark 8:27-30, also Matthew 16:13-20, Luke 9:18-21).

[See Lessons: **Jesus teaches about himself**.]

Jesus reveals he will be killed by religious leaders

[Jesus] began to teach them that the Son of Man must suffer many things, and be rejected by the elders, the chief priests, and the scribes, and be killed, and after three days rise again. He spoke to them openly. Peter took him, and began to rebuke him. But he, turning around, and seeing his disciples, rebuked Peter, and said, "Get behind me, Satan! For you have in mind not the things of God, but the things of men" (Mark 8:31-33, also Matthew 16:21-26, Luke 9:22-25).

Jesus reveals cost of following him

He called the multitude to himself with his disciples, and said to them, "Whoever wants to come after me, let him deny himself, and take up his cross, and follow me. For whoever wants to save his life will lose it; and whoever will lose his life for my sake and the sake of the Good News will save it. For what does it profit a man, to gain the whole world, and forfeit his life? For what will a man give in exchange for his life? For whoever will be ashamed of me and of my words in this adulterous and sinful generation, the Son of Man also will be ashamed of him, when he comes in his Father's glory, with the holy angels."

He said to them, "Most certainly I tell you, there are some standing here who will in no way taste death until they see God's Kingdom come with power" (Mark 8:34-9:1, also Matthew 16:21-26, Luke 9:22-27).

Jesus is transfigured

About eight days after these sayings, he took with him Peter, John, and James, and went up onto the mountain to pray. As he was praying, the appearance of his face was altered, and his clothing became white and dazzling. Behold, two men were talking with him, who were Moses and Elijah, who appeared in glory, and spoke of his departure, which he was about to accomplish at Jerusalem.

Now Peter and those who were with him were heavy with sleep, but when they were fully awake, they saw his glory, and the two men who stood with him. As they were parting from him, Peter said to Jesus, "Master, it is good for us to be here. Let's make three tents: one for you, and one for Moses, and one for Elijah," not knowing what he said.

While he said these things, a cloud came and overshadowed them, and they were afraid as they entered into the cloud. A voice came out of the cloud, saying, "This is my beloved Son. Listen to him!" When the voice came, Jesus was found alone. They were silent, and told no one in those days any of the things which they had seen (Luke 9:28-36, also Matthew 17:1-8, also Mark 9:2-8).

As they were coming down from the mountain, he commanded them that they should tell no one what things they had seen, until after the Son of Man had risen from the dead. They kept this saying to themselves, questioning what the "rising from the dead" meant.

They asked him, saying, "Why do the scribes say that Elijah must come first?"

He said to them, "Elijah indeed comes first, and restores all things. How is it written about the Son of Man, that he should suffer many things and be despised? But I tell you that Elijah has come, and they have also done to him whatever they wanted to, even as it is written about him" (Mark 9:9-13, also Matthew 17:9-13).

Jesus heals demon-possessed boy

Coming to the disciples, [Jesus] saw a great multitude around them, and scribes questioning them. Immediately all the multitude, when they saw him, were greatly amazed, and running to him greeted him. He asked the scribes, "What are you asking them?"

One of the multitude answered, "Teacher, I brought to you my son, who has a mute spirit; and wherever it seizes him, it throws him down, and he foams at the mouth, and grinds his teeth and wastes away. I asked your disciples to cast it out, and they weren't able."

He answered him, "Unbelieving generation, how long shall I be with you? How long shall I bear with you? Bring him to me."

They brought him to him, and when he saw him, immediately the spirit convulsed him, and he fell on the ground, wallowing and foaming at the mouth.

He asked his father, "How long has it been since this has come to him?"

He said, "From childhood. Often it has cast him both into the fire and into the water to destroy him. But if you can do anything, have compassion on us, and help us."

Jesus said to him, "If you can believe, all things are possible to him who believes."

Immediately the father of the child cried out with tears, "I believe. Help my unbelief!"

When Jesus saw that a multitude came running together, he rebuked the unclean spirit, saying to him, "You mute and deaf spirit, I command you, come out of him, and never enter him again!"

Having cried out, and convulsed greatly, it came out of him. The boy became like one dead; so much that most of them said, "He is dead." But Jesus took him by the hand, and raised him up; and he arose.

When he had come into the house, his disciples asked him privately, "Why couldn't we cast it out?" He said to them, "This kind can come out by nothing, except by prayer and fasting" (Mark 9:14-29, also Matthew 17:14-19, Luke 9:37-43a).

"For most certainly I tell you, if you have faith as a grain of mustard seed, you will tell this mountain, 'Move from here to there,' and it will move; and nothing will be impossible for you. But this kind doesn't go out except by prayer and fasting" (Matthew 17:20-21).

Jesus again predicts his death

While they were staying in Galilee, Jesus said to them, "The Son of Man is about to be delivered up into the hands of men, and they will kill him, and the third day he will be raised up." They were exceedingly sorry (Matthew 17:22-23, also Mark 9:30-32, Luke 9:4eb-45).

Jesus questioned about paying taxes

When [the disciples] had come to Capernaum, those who collected the [tax] coins came to Peter, and said, "Doesn't your teacher pay the [tax]?" He said, "Yes."

When he came into the house, Jesus anticipated him, saying, "What do you think, Simon? From whom do the kings of the earth receive toll or tribute? From their children, or from strangers?"

Peter said to him, "From strangers."

Jesus said to him, "Therefore the children are exempt. But, lest we cause them to stumble, go to the sea, cast a hook, and take up the first fish that comes up. When you have opened its mouth, you will find a [tax] coin. Take that, and give it to them for me and you" (Matthew 17:24-27).

Jesus travels to feast in Jerusalem

Now the feast of the Jews, the Feast of Booths, was at hand. [Jesus'] brothers therefore said to him, "Depart from here, and go into Judea, that your disciples also may see your works which you do. For no one does anything in secret, and himself seeks to be known openly. If you do these things, reveal yourself to the world." For even his brothers didn't believe in him.

Jesus therefore said to them, "My time has not yet come, but your time is always ready. The world can't hate you, but it hates me, because I testify about it, that its works are evil. You go up to the feast. I am not yet going up to this feast, because my time is not yet fulfilled."

Having said these things to them, he stayed in Galilee. But when his brothers had gone up to the feast, then he also went up, not publicly, but as it were in secret (John 7:2-10).

Jesus sets face toward Jerusalem

It came to pass, when the days were near that he should be taken up, he intently set his face to go to Jerusalem, and sent messengers before his face. They went, and entered into a village of the Samaritans, so as to prepare for him. They didn't receive him, because he was traveling with his face set toward Jerusalem. When his disciples, James and John, saw this, they said, "Lord, do you want us to command fire to come down from the sky, and destroy them, just as Elijah did?"

But he turned and rebuked them, "You don't know of what kind of spirit you are. For the Son of Man didn't come to destroy men's lives, but to save them" (Luke 9:51-55).

The cost of following Jesus

[Jesus and his disciples] went to another village. As they went on the way, a certain man said to him, "I want to follow you wherever you go, Lord."

Jesus said to him, "The foxes have holes, and the birds of the sky have nests, but the Son of Man has no place to lay his head."

He said to another, "Follow me!"

But he said, "Lord, allow me first to go and bury my father."

But Jesus said to him, "Leave the dead to bury their own dead, but you go and announce God's Kingdom."

Another also said, "I want to follow you, Lord, but first allow me to say good-bye to those who are at my house."

But Jesus said to him, "No one, having put his hand to the plow, and looking back, is fit for God's Kingdom" (Luke 9:56-62, also Matthew 8:19-22).

Jesus creates division in Jerusalem

The Jews therefore sought [Jesus] at the feast, and said, "Where is he?" There was much murmuring among the multitudes concerning him. Some said, "He is a good man." Others said, "Not so, but he leads the multitude astray." Yet no one spoke openly of him for fear of the Jews. But when it was now the middle of the feast, Jesus went up into the temple and taught. The Jews therefore marveled, saying, "How does this man know letters, having never been educated?"

Jesus therefore answered them, "My teaching is not mine, but his who sent me. If anyone desires to do his will, he will know about the teaching, whether it is from God, or if I am speaking from myself. He who speaks from himself seeks his own glory, but he who seeks the glory of him who sent him is true, and no unrighteousness is in him. Didn't Moses give you the law, and yet none of you keeps the law? Why do you seek to kill me?"

The multitude answered, "You have a demon! Who seeks to kill you?"

Jesus answered them, "I did one work, and you all marvel because of it. Moses has given you circumcision (not that it is of Moses, but of the fathers), and on the Sabbath you circumcise a boy. If a boy receives circumcision on the Sabbath, that the law of Moses may not be broken, are you angry with me, because I made a man completely healthy on the Sabbath? Don't judge according to appearance, but judge righteous judgment."

Therefore some of them of Jerusalem said, "Isn't this he whom they seek to kill? Behold, he speaks openly, and they say nothing to him. Can it be that the rulers indeed know that this is truly the Christ? However we know where this man comes from, but when the Christ comes, no one will know where he comes from."

Jesus therefore cried out in the temple, teaching and saying, "You both know me, and know where I am from. I have not come of myself, but he who sent me is true, whom you don't know. I know him, because I am from him, and he sent me."

They sought therefore to take him; but no one laid a hand on him, because his hour had not yet come. But of the multitude, many believed in him. They said, "When the Christ comes, he won't do more signs than those which this man has done, will he?" The Pharisees heard the multitude murmuring these things concerning him, and the chief priests and the Pharisees sent officers to arrest him.

Then Jesus said, "I will be with you a little while longer, then I go to him who sent me. You will seek me and won't find me; and where I am, you can't come."

The Jews therefore said among themselves, "Where will this man go that we won't find him? Will he go to the Dispersion among the Greeks, and teach the Greeks? What is this word that he said, 'You will seek me, and won't find me; and where I am, you can't come'?"

Now on the last and greatest day of the feast, Jesus stood and cried out, "If anyone is thirsty, let him come to me and drink! He who believes in me, as the Scripture has said, from within him will flow rivers of living water." But he said this about the Spirit, which those believing in him were to receive. For the Holy Spirit was not yet given, because Jesus wasn't yet glorified.

Many of the multitude therefore, when they heard these words, said, "This is truly the prophet." Others said, "This is the Christ." But some said, "What, does the Christ come out of Galilee? Hasn't the Scripture said that the Christ comes of the offspring of David, and from Bethlehem, the village where David was?" So there arose a division in the multitude because of him. Some of them would have arrested him, but no one laid hands on him. The officers therefore came to the chief priests and Pharisees, and they said to them, "Why didn't you bring him?"

The officers answered, "No man ever spoke like this man!"

The Pharisees therefore answered them, "You aren't also led astray, are you? Have any of the rulers believed in him, or of the Pharisees? But this multitude that doesn't know the law is accursed."

Nicodemus (he who came to him by night, being one of them) said to them, "Does our law judge a man, unless it first hears from him personally and knows what he does?"

They answered him, "Are you also from Galilee? Search, and see that no prophet has arisen out of Galilee" (John 7:11-52).

Many believe in Jesus

Jesus therefore said to them, "When you have lifted up the Son of Man, then you will know that I am he, and I do nothing of myself, but as my Father taught me, I say these things. He who sent me is with me. The Father hasn't left me alone, for I always do the things that are pleasing to him."

As he spoke these things, many believed in him (John 8:28-30).

[See Lessons: **Jesus teaches about himself** (John 8:31-58).]

The Jews attempt to stone Jesus

Therefore they took up stones to throw at him, but Jesus was hidden, and went out of the temple, having gone through the middle of them, and so passed by (John 8:59).

Jesus heals a blind man, divides religious leaders

As [Jesus] passed by, he saw a man blind from birth. His disciples asked him, "Rabbi, who sinned, this man or his parents, that he was born blind?"

Jesus answered, "Neither did this man sin, nor his parents; but, that the works of God might be revealed in him. I must work the works of him who sent me, while it is day. The night is coming, when no one can work. While I am in the world, I am the light of the world." When he had said this, he spat on the ground, made mud with the saliva, anointed the blind man's eyes with the mud, and said to him, "Go, wash in the pool of Siloam" (which means "Sent"). So he went away, washed, and came back seeing. The neighbors therefore, and those who saw that he was blind before, said, "Isn't this he who sat and begged?" Others were saying, "It is he." Still others were saying, "He looks like him."

He said, "I am he." They therefore were asking him, "How were your eyes opened?"

He answered, "A man called Jesus made mud, anointed my eyes, and said to me, 'Go to the pool of Siloam, and wash.' So I went away and washed, and I received sight."

Then they asked him, "Where is he?"

He said, "I don't know.

They brought him who had been blind to the Pharisees. It was a Sabbath when Jesus made the mud and opened his eyes. Again therefore the Pharisees also asked him how he received his sight. He said to them, "He put mud on my eyes, I washed, and I see."

Some therefore of the Pharisees said, "This man is not from God, because he doesn't keep the Sabbath." Others said, "How can a man who is a sinner do such signs?" There was division among them. Therefore they asked the blind man again, "What do you say about him, because he opened your eyes?"

He said, "He is a prophet."

The Jews therefore did not believe concerning him, that he had been blind, and had received his sight, until they called the parents of him who had received his sight, and asked them, "Is this your son, whom you say was born blind? How then does he now see?"

His parents answered them, "We know that this is our son, and that he was born blind; but how he now sees, we don't know; or who opened his eyes, we don't know. He is of age. Ask him. He will speak for himself." His parents said these things because they feared the Jews; for the Jews had already agreed that if any man would confess him as Christ, he would be put out of the synagogue. Therefore his parents said, "He is of age. Ask him."

So they called the man who was blind a second time, and said to him, "Give glory to God. We know that this man is a sinner."

He therefore answered, "I don't know if he is a sinner. One thing I do know: that though I was blind, now I see."

They said to him again, "What did he do to you? How did he open your eyes?"

He answered them, "I told you already, and you didn't listen. Why do you want to hear it again? You don't also want to become his disciples, do you?"

They insulted him and said, "You are his disciple, but we are disciples of Moses. We know that God has spoken to Moses. But as for this man, we don't know where he comes from."

The man answered them, "How amazing! You don't know where he comes from, yet he opened my eyes. We know that God doesn't listen to sinners, but if anyone is a worshiper of God, and does his will, he listens to him. Since the world began it has never been heard of that anyone opened the eyes of someone born blind. If this man were not from God, he could do nothing."

They answered him, "You were altogether born in sins, and do you teach us?" They threw him out.

Jesus heard that they had thrown him out, and finding him, he said, "Do you believe in the Son of God?"

He answered, "Who is he, Lord, that I may believe in him?"

Jesus said to him, "You have both seen him, and it is he who speaks with you."

He said, "Lord, I believe!" and he worshiped him.

Jesus said, "I came into this world for judgment, that those who don't see may see; and that those who see may become blind."

Those of the Pharisees who were with him heard these things, and said to him, "Are we also blind?"

Jesus said to them, "If you were blind, you would have no sin; but now you say, 'We see.' Therefore your sin remains" (John 9:1-41).

Jesus sends out seventy disciples

Now after these things, the Lord also appointed seventy others, and sent them two by two ahead of him into every city and place, where he was about to come. Then he said to them, "The harvest is indeed plentiful, but the laborers are few. Pray therefore to the Lord of the harvest, that he may send out laborers into his harvest. Go your ways. Behold, I send you out as lambs among wolves. Carry no purse, nor wallet, nor sandals. Greet no one on the way. Into whatever house you enter, first say, 'Peace be to this house.' If a son of peace is there, your peace will rest on him; but if not, it will return to you. Remain in that same house, eating and drinking the things they give, for the laborer is worthy of his wages. Don't go from house to house. Into whatever city you enter, and they receive you, eat the things that are set before you. Heal the sick who are therein, and tell them, 'God's Kingdom has come near to you.' But into whatever city you enter, and they don't receive you, go out into its streets and say, 'Even the dust from your city that clings to us, we wipe off against you. Nevertheless know this, that God's Kingdom has come near to you.' I tell you, it will be more tolerable in that day for Sodom than for that city.

"Woe to you, Chorazin! Woe to you, Bethsaida! For if the mighty works had been done in Tyre and Sidon which were done in you, they would have repented long ago, sitting in sackcloth and ashes. But it will be more tolerable for Tyre and Sidon in the judgment than for you. You, Capernaum, who are exalted to heaven, will be brought down to Hades. Whoever listens to you listens to me, and whoever rejects you rejects me. Whoever rejects me rejects him who sent me."

The seventy returned with joy, saying, "Lord, even the demons are subject to us in your name!"

He said to them, "I saw Satan having fallen like lightning from heaven. Behold, I give you authority to tread on serpents and scorpions, and over all the power of the enemy. Nothing will in any way hurt you. Nevertheless, don't rejoice in this, that the spirits are subject to you, but rejoice that your names are written in heaven."

In that same hour Jesus rejoiced in the Holy Spirit, and said, "I thank you, O Father, Lord of heaven and earth, that you have hidden these things from the wise and understanding, and revealed them to little children. Yes, Father, for so it was well-pleasing in your sight."

Turning to the disciples, he said, "All things have been delivered to me by my Father. No one knows who the Son is, except the Father, and who the Father is, except the Son, and he to whomever the Son desires to reveal him."

Turning to the disciples, he said privately, "Blessed are the eyes which see the things that you see, for I tell you that many prophets and kings desired to see the things which you see, and didn't see them, and to hear the things which you hear, and didn't hear them" (Luke 10:1-24).

Jesus teaches about eternal life

Behold, a certain lawyer stood up and tested him, saying, "Teacher, what shall I do to inherit eternal life?"(Luke 10:25).

[See Lessons: **Eternal life** (Luke10:25-37).]

Jesus teaches about priorities

As they went on their way, he entered into a certain village, and a certain woman named Martha received him into her house. She had a sister called Mary, who also sat at Jesus' feet, and heard his word. But Martha was distracted with much serving, and she came up to him, and said, "Lord, don't you care that my sister left me to serve alone? Ask her therefore to help me."

Jesus answered her, "Martha, Martha, you are anxious and troubled about many things, but one thing is needed. Mary has chosen the good part, which will not be taken away from her." (Luke 10:38-42).

Jesus confronts the Pharisees

Now as he spoke, a certain Pharisee asked him to dine with him. He went in, and sat at the table. When the Pharisee saw it, he marveled that he had not first washed himself before dinner. The Lord said to him, "Now you Pharisees cleanse the outside of the cup and of the platter, but your inward part is full of extortion and wickedness. You foolish ones, didn't he who made the outside make the inside also? But give for gifts to the needy those things which are within, and behold, all things will be clean to you. But woe to you Pharisees! For you tithe mint and rue and every herb, but you bypass justice and the love of God. You ought to have done these and not to have left the other undone. Woe to you Pharisees! For you love the best seats in the synagogues and the greetings in the marketplaces. Woe to you, scribes and Pharisees, hypocrites! For you are like hidden graves, and the men who walk over them don't know it."

One of the lawyers answered him, "Teacher, in saying this you insult us also."

He said, "Woe to you lawyers also! For you load men with burdens that are difficult to carry, and you yourselves won't even lift one finger to help carry those burdens. Woe to you! For you build the tombs of the prophets, and your fathers killed them. So you testify and consent to the works of your fathers. For they killed them, and you build their tombs. Therefore also the wisdom of God said, 'I will send to them prophets and apostles; and some of them they will kill and persecute, that the blood of all the prophets, which was shed from the foundation of the world, may be required of this generation; from the blood of Abel to the blood of Zachariah, who perished between the altar and the sanctuary.' Yes, I tell you, it will be required of this generation. Woe to you lawyers! For you took away the key of knowledge. You didn't enter in yourselves, and those who were entering in, you hindered."

As he said these things to them, the scribes and the Pharisees began to be terribly angry, and to draw many things out of him; lying in wait for him, and seeking to catch him in something he might say, that they might accuse him (Luke 11:37-53).

Jesus teaches thousands

Meanwhile, when a multitude of many thousands had gathered together, so much so that they trampled on each other, he began to [teach] (Luke 12:1).

[See Lessons: **Anxiety, End times, Hypocrisy, Riches, Persecution** (Luke 12:1-59.]

Jesus heals crippled woman on Sabbath

He was teaching in one of the synagogues on the Sabbath day. Behold, there was a woman who had a spirit of infirmity eighteen years, and she was bent over and could in no way straighten herself up. When Jesus saw her, he called her and said to her, "Woman, you are freed from your infirmity." He laid his hands on her, and immediately she stood up straight and glorified God.

The ruler of the synagogue, being indignant because Jesus had healed on the Sabbath, said to the multitude, "There are six days in which men ought to work. Therefore come on those days and be healed and not on the Sabbath day!"

Therefore the Lord answered him, "You hypocrites! Doesn't each one of you free his ox or his donkey from the stall on the Sabbath and lead him away to water? Ought not this woman, being a daughter of Abraham whom Satan had bound eighteen long years, be freed from this bondage on the Sabbath day?"

As he said these things, all his adversaries were disappointed, and all the multitude rejoiced for all the glorious things that were done by him (Luke 13:10-17).

Religious leaders again attempt to stone Jesus

It was the Feast of the Dedication at Jerusalem. It was winter, and Jesus was walking in the temple, in Solomon's porch. The Jews therefore came around him and said to him, "How long will you hold us in suspense? If you are the Christ, tell us plainly."

Jesus answered them, "I told you, and you don't believe. The works that I do in my Father's name, these testify about me. But you don't believe, because you are not of my sheep, as I told you. My sheep hear my voice, and I know them, and they follow me. I give eternal life to them. They will never perish, and no one will snatch them out of my hand. My Father, who has given them to me, is greater than all. No one is able to snatch them out of my Father's hand. I and the Father are one."

Therefore Jews took up stones again to stone him. Jesus answered them, "I have shown you many good works from my Father. For which of those works do you stone me?"

The Jews answered him, "We don't stone you for a good work, but for blasphemy: because you, being a man, make yourself God."

Jesus answered them, "Isn't it written in your law, 'I said, you are gods?' If he called them gods, to whom the word of God came (and the Scripture can't be broken), do you say of him whom the Father sanctified and sent into the world, 'You blaspheme,' because I said, 'I am the Son of God?' If I don't do the works of my Father, don't believe me. But if I do them, though you don't believe me, believe the works; that you may know and believe that the Father is in me, and I in the Father."

They sought again to seize him, and he went out of their hand. He went away again beyond the Jordan into the place where John was baptizing at first, and there he stayed. Many came to him. They said, "John indeed did no sign, but everything that John said about this man is true." Many believed in him there (John 10:22-42).

Jesus confronts his critics

He went on his way through cities and villages, teaching and traveling on to Jerusalem. One said to him, "Lord, are they few who are saved?"

He said to them, "Strive to enter in by the narrow door, for many, I tell you, will seek to enter in and will not be able. When once the master of the house has risen up and has shut the door, and you begin to stand outside and to knock at the door, saying, 'Lord, Lord, open to us!' then he will answer and tell you, 'I don't know you or where you come from.' Then you will begin to say, 'We ate and drank in your presence, and you taught in our streets.' He will say, 'I tell you, I don't know where you come from. Depart from me, all you workers of iniquity.' There will be weeping and gnashing of teeth, when you see Abraham, Isaac, Jacob, and all the prophets in God's Kingdom and yourselves being thrown outside. They will come from the east, west, north, and south and will sit down in God's Kingdom. Behold, there are some who are last who will be first, and there are some who are first who will be last."

On that same day, some Pharisees came, saying to him, "Get out of here, and go away, for Herod wants to kill you."

He said to them, "Go and tell that fox, 'Behold, I cast out demons and perform cures today and tomorrow, and the third day I complete my mission. Nevertheless I must go on my way today and tomorrow and the next day, for it can't be that a prophet perish outside of Jerusalem.'

"Jerusalem, Jerusalem, that kills the prophets, and stones those who are sent to her! How often I wanted to gather your children together, like a hen gathers her own brood under her wings, and you refused! Behold, your house is left to you desolate. I tell you, you will not see me, until you say, 'Blessed is he who comes in the name of the Lord!'" (Luke 13:22-35).

Jesus heals man with dropsy on Sabbath

When he went into the house of one of the rulers of the Pharisees on a Sabbath to eat bread, they were watching him. Behold, a certain man who had dropsy was in front of him. Jesus answering, spoke to the lawyers and Pharisees saying, "Is it lawful to heal on the Sabbath?"

But they were silent.

He took him, and healed him, and let him go. He answered them, "Which of you, if your son or an ox fell into a well, wouldn't immediately pull him out on a Sabbath day?"

They couldn't answer him regarding these things (Luke 14:1-6).

Jesus confronts Pharisees and scribes

Now all the tax collectors and sinners were coming close to him to hear him. The Pharisees and the scribes murmured saying, "This man welcomes sinners, and eats with them" (Luke 15:1-2).

[See Lessons: **Parable of lost sheep and coin, Parable of lost son** (Luke 15:3-32), **Parable of dishonest manager** (Luke 16:1-13).]

Jesus raises Lazarus from tomb

Now a certain man was sick, Lazarus from Bethany, of the village of Mary and her sister, Martha. It was that Mary who had anointed the Lord with ointment, and wiped his feet with her hair, whose brother, Lazarus, was sick. The sisters therefore sent to him, saying, "Lord, behold, he for whom you have great affection is sick." But when Jesus heard it, he said, "This sickness is not to death, but for the glory of God, that God's Son may be glorified by it." Now Jesus loved Martha, and her sister, and Lazarus. When therefore he heard that he was sick, he stayed two days in the place where he was. Then after this he said to the disciples, "Let's go into Judea again."

The disciples told him, "Rabbi, the Jews were just trying to stone you, and are you going there again?"

Jesus answered, "Aren't there twelve hours of daylight? If a man walks in the day, he doesn't stumble, because he sees the light of this world. But if a man walks in the night, he stumbles, because the light isn't in him." He said these things, and after that, he said to them, "Our friend, Lazarus, has fallen asleep, but I am going so that I may awake him out of sleep."

The disciples therefore said, "Lord, if he has fallen asleep, he will recover."

Now Jesus had spoken of his death, but they thought that he spoke of taking rest in sleep. So Jesus said to them plainly then,

"Lazarus is dead. I am glad for your sakes that I was not there, so that you may believe. Nevertheless, let's go to him."

Thomas therefore, who is called Didymus, said to his fellow disciples, "Let's go also, that we may die with him."

So when Jesus came, he found that [Lazarus] had been in the tomb four days already. Now Bethany was near Jerusalem, [less than two miles] away. Many of the Jews had joined the women around Martha and Mary, to console them concerning their brother. Then when Martha heard that Jesus was coming, she went and met him, but Mary stayed in the house. Therefore Martha said to Jesus, "Lord, if you would have been here, my brother wouldn't have died. Even now I know that, whatever you ask of God, God will give you." Jesus said to her, "Your brother will rise again."

Martha said to him, "I know that he will rise again in the resurrection at the last day."

Jesus said to her, "I am the resurrection and the life. He who believes in me will still live, even if he dies. Whoever lives and believes in me will never die. Do you believe this?"

She said to him, "Yes, Lord. I have come to believe that you are the Christ, God's Son, he who comes into the world."

When she had said this, she went away and called Mary, her sister, secretly, saying, "The Teacher is here, and is calling you."

When she heard this, she arose quickly and went to him. Now Jesus had not yet come into the village, but was in the place where Martha met him. Then the Jews who were with her in the house, and were consoling her, when they saw Mary, that she rose up quickly and went out, followed her, saying, "She is going to the tomb to weep there." Therefore when Mary came to where Jesus was and saw him, she fell down at his feet, saying to him, "Lord, if you would have been here, my brother wouldn't have died."

When Jesus therefore saw her weeping, and the Jews weeping who came with her, he groaned in the spirit and was troubled, and said, "Where have you laid him?"

They told him, "Lord, come and see."

Jesus wept.

The Jews therefore said, "See how much affection he had for him!" Some of them said, "Couldn't this man, who opened the eyes of him who was blind, have also kept this man from dying?"

Jesus therefore, again groaning in himself, came to the tomb. Now it was a cave, and a stone lay against it. Jesus said, "Take away the stone."

Martha, the sister of him who was dead, said to him, "Lord, by this time there is a stench, for he has been dead four days."

Jesus said to her, "Didn't I tell you that if you believed, you would see God's glory?"

So they took away the stone from the place where the dead man was lying. Jesus lifted up his eyes and said, "Father, I thank you that you listened to me. I know that you always listen to me, but because of the multitude that stands around I said this, that they may believe that you sent me." When he had said this, he cried with a loud voice, "Lazarus, come out!"

He who was dead came out, bound hand and foot with wrappings, and his face was wrapped around with a cloth.

Jesus said to them, "Free him, and let him go."

Therefore many of the Jews, who came to Mary and saw what Jesus did, believed in him. But some of them went away to the Pharisees and told them the things which Jesus had done (John 11:1-46).

Chief priests and Pharisees conspire to kill Jesus

The chief priests therefore and the Pharisees gathered a council and said, "What are we doing? For this man does many signs. If we leave him alone like this, everyone will believe in him, and the Romans will come and take away both our place and our nation."

But a certain one of them, Caiaphas, being high priest that year, said to them, "You know nothing at all, nor do you consider that it is advantageous for us that one man should die for the people and that the whole nation not perish." Now he didn't say this of himself, but being high priest that year, he prophesied that Jesus would die for the nation, and not for the nation only, but that he might also gather together into one the children of God who are scattered abroad. So from that day forward, they took counsel that they might put him to death. Jesus therefore walked no more openly among the Jews, but departed from there into the country near the wilderness, to a city called Ephraim. He stayed there with his disciples (John 11:47-54, also Matthew 26:1-5, Mark 14:1-2, Luke 22:1-2).

Jesus heals ten men with leprosy
As he was on his way to Jerusalem, he was passing along the borders of Samaria and Galilee. As he entered into a certain village, ten men who were lepers met him, who stood at a distance. They lifted up their voices, saying, "Jesus, Master, have mercy on us!"

When he saw them, he said to them, "Go and show yourselves to the priests." As they went, they were cleansed. One of them, when he saw that he was healed, turned back, glorifying God with a loud voice. He fell on his face at Jesus' feet, giving him thanks; and he was a Samaritan. Jesus answered, "Weren't the ten cleansed? But where are the nine? Were there none found who returned to give glory to God, except this stranger?" Then he said to him, "Get up, and go your way. Your faith has healed you" (Luke 17:11-19).

Jesus teaches about Kingdom of heaven, End of the age
Being asked by the Pharisees when God's Kingdom would come, [Jesus] answered them, "God's Kingdom doesn't come with observation; neither will they say, 'Look, here!' or, 'Look, there!' for behold, God's Kingdom is within you" (Luke 17:20-21).

[See Lessons: **End of the Age** (Luke 17:22-37).]

Jesus continues to teach disciples
[See Lessons: **Prayer** (Luke 18:1-8), **Humility** (Luke 18:9-14), **Children** (Luke 18:15-17), **Eternal life** (Luke 18:17-27).

Jesus travels to Judea, heals and teaches there
When Jesus had finished these words, he departed from Galilee, and came into the borders of Judea beyond the Jordan. Great multitudes followed him, and he healed them there (Matthew 19:1-2).

[See Lessons: **Divorce** (Matthew 19:3-12, also Mark 10:2-12)].

71

Jesus predicts his crucifixion

As Jesus was going up to Jerusalem, he took the twelve disciples aside, and on the way he said to them, "Behold, we are going up to Jerusalem, and the Son of Man will be delivered to the chief priests and scribes, and they will condemn him to death, and will hand him over to the Gentiles to mock, to scourge, and to crucify; and the third day he will be raised up" (Matthew 20:17-19, also Mark 10:32-34, Luke 18:31-34).

James and John's mother asks for special recognition

Then the mother of the sons of Zebedee came to him with her sons, kneeling and asking a certain thing of him. He said to her, "What do you want?"

She said to him, "Command that these, my two sons, may sit, one on your right hand and one on your left hand, in your Kingdom."

But Jesus answered, "You don't know what you are asking. Are you able to drink the cup that I am about to drink and be baptized with the baptism that I am baptized with?"

They said to him, "We are able."

He said to them, "You will indeed drink my cup and be baptized with the baptism that I am baptized with, but to sit on my right hand and on my left hand is not mine to give; but it is for whom it has been prepared by my Father."

When the ten heard it, they were indignant with the two brothers.

But Jesus summoned them, and said, "You know that the rulers of the nations lord it over them, and their great ones exercise authority over them. It shall not be so among you, but whoever desires to become great among you shall be your servant. Whoever desires to be first among you shall be your bondservant, even as the Son of Man came not to be served, but to serve and to give his life as a ransom for many" (Matthew 20:20-28, also Mark 10:35-45).

Jesus heals two blind men

As [Jesus] went out from Jericho with his disciples and a great multitude, the son of Timaeus, Bartimaeus, a blind beggar, was sitting by the road. When he heard that it was Jesus the Nazarene, he began to cry out and say, "Jesus, you son of David, have mercy on me!" Many rebuked him, that he should be quiet, but he cried out much more, "You son of David, have mercy on me!"

Jesus stood still and said, "Call him."

They called the blind man, saying to him, "Cheer up! Get up. He is calling you!"

He, casting away his cloak, sprang up and came to Jesus.

Jesus asked him, "What do you want me to do for you?"

The blind man said to him, "Master, that I may see again."

Jesus said to him, "Go your way. Your faith has made you well." Immediately he received his sight and followed Jesus on the way (Mark 10:46-52, also Matthew 20:29-34, Luke 18:35-43).

Zaccheus follows Jesus

[Jesus] entered and was passing through Jericho. There was a man named Zacchaeus. He was a chief tax collector, and he was rich. He was trying to see who Jesus was and couldn't because of the crowd, because he was short. He ran on ahead, and climbed up into a sycamore tree to see him, for he was going to pass that way. When Jesus came to the place, he looked up and saw him, and said to him, "Zacchaeus, hurry and come down, for today I must stay at your house." He hurried, came down, and received him joyfully. When they saw it, they all murmured, saying, "He has gone in to lodge with a man who is a sinner."

Zacchaeus stood and said to the Lord, "Behold, Lord, half of my goods I give to the poor. If I have wrongfully exacted anything of anyone, I restore four times as much."

Jesus said to him, "Today, salvation has come to this house, because he also is a son of Abraham. For the Son of Man came to seek and to save that which was lost" (Luke 19:1-10).

Jesus tells parable about being a good steward

As they heard these things, he went on and told a parable, because he was near Jerusalem, and they supposed that God's Kingdom would be revealed immediately (Luke 19:11).

[See Lessons: **Stewardship** (Luke 19:11-28).]

Jesus becomes wanted man

Jesus . . . walked no more openly among the Jews, but departed from there into the country near the wilderness, to a city called Ephraim. He stayed there with his disciples.

Now the Passover of the Jews was at hand. Many went up from the country to Jerusalem before the Passover to purify themselves. Then they sought for Jesus and spoke one with another, as they stood in the temple, "What do you think—that he isn't coming to the feast at all?" Now the chief priests and the Pharisees had commanded that if anyone knew where he was, he should report it, that they might seize him (John 11:54-57).

Mary anoints Jesus with expensive ointment

Then six days before the Passover, Jesus came to Bethany, where Lazarus was, who had been dead, whom he raised from the dead. So they made him a supper there. Martha served, but Lazarus was one of those who sat at the table with him. Mary, therefore, took a pound of ointment of pure nard, very precious, and anointed the feet of Jesus, and wiped his feet with her hair. The house was filled with the fragrance of the ointment. Then Judas Iscariot, Simon's son, one of his disciples, who would betray him, said, "Why wasn't this ointment sold for [nearly a year's wages] and given to the poor?" Now he said this, not because he cared for the poor, but because he was a thief, and having the money box, used to steal what was put into it. But Jesus said, "Leave her alone. She has kept this for the day of my burial. For you always have the poor with you, but you don't always have me" (John 12:1-8, also Matthew 26:6-12, Mark 14:3-8).

"Most certainly I tell you, wherever this Good News is preached in the whole world, what this woman has done will also be spoken of as a memorial of her" (Matthew 26:13, also Mark 14:9).

A large crowd . . . of the Jews learned that he was there, and they came, not for Jesus' sake only, but that they might see Lazarus also, whom he had raised from the dead. But the chief priests conspired to put Lazarus to death also, because on account of him many of the Jews went away and believed in Jesus (John 12:9-11).

When he came near to Bethsphage and Bethany, at the mountain that is called Olivet, he sent two of his disciples saying, "Go your way into the village on the other side, in which, as you enter, you will find a colt tied, whereon no man ever yet sat. Untie it, and bring it. If anyone asks you, 'Why are you untying it?' say to him: 'The Lord needs it.'"

Those who were sent went away and found things just as he had told them. As they were untying the colt, its owners said to them, "Why are you untying the colt?" They said, "The Lord needs it." They brought it to Jesus. They threw their cloaks on the colt and set Jesus on them (Luke 19:29-35, also Matthew 21:1-11, Mark 11:1-11, John 12:12-19).

All this was done, that it might be fulfilled which was spoken through the prophet, saying,

> "Tell the daughter of Zion,
> behold, your King comes to you,
> humble, and riding on a donkey,
> on a colt, the foal of a donkey" (Matthew 21:4-5).

As he went, they spread their cloaks on the road. As he was now getting near, at the descent of the Mount of Olives, the whole multitude of the disciples began to rejoice and praise God with a loud voice for all the mighty works which they had seen, saying, "Blessed is the King who comes in the name of the Lord! Peace in heaven, and glory in the highest!"

Some of the Pharisees from the multitude said to him, "Teacher, rebuke your disciples!"

He answered them, "I tell you that if these were silent, the stones would cry out."

When he came near, he saw the city and wept over it, saying, "If you, even you, had known today the things which belong to your peace! But now, they are hidden from your eyes. For the days will come on you, when your enemies will throw up a barricade against you, surround you, hem you in on every side, and will dash you and your children within you to the ground. They will not leave in you one stone on another, because you didn't know the time of your visitation" (Luke 19:36-44).

Jesus entered into the temple in Jerusalem. When he had looked around at everything, it being now evening, he went out to Bethany with the twelve (Mark 11:11).

Jesus curses fig tree

The next day, when they had come out from Bethany, he was hungry. Seeing a fig tree afar off having leaves, he came to see if perhaps he might find anything on it. When he came to it, he found nothing but leaves, for it was not the season for figs. Jesus told it, "May no one ever eat fruit from you again!" and his disciples heard it (Mark 11:12-13).

Jesus clears Temple

The Passover of the Jews was at hand, and Jesus went up to Jerusalem. He found in the temple those who sold oxen, sheep, and doves, and the changers of money sitting. He made a whip of cords, and threw all out of the temple, both the sheep and the oxen; and he poured out the changers' money, and overthrew their tables. To those who sold the doves, he said, "Take these things out of here! Don't make my Father's house a marketplace!" His disciples remembered that it was written, "Zeal for your house will eat me up" (John 2:13-17, also Matthew 21:12-13, Mark 11:15, Luke 19:45-46).

He would not allow anyone to carry a container through the temple. He taught, saying to them, "Isn't it written, 'My house will be called a house of prayer for all the nations?' But you have made it a den of robbers!"

The chief priests and the scribes heard it and sought how they might destroy him. For they feared him, because all the multitude was astonished at his teaching (Mark 11:16-18).

Cursed fig tree is withered, Jesus teaches about faith

When evening came, he went out of the city. As they passed by in the morning, they saw the fig tree withered away from the roots. Peter, remembering, said to him, "Rabbi, look! The fig tree which you cursed has withered away."

Jesus answered them, "Have faith in God. For most certainly I tell you, whoever may tell this mountain, 'Be taken up and cast into the sea' and doesn't doubt in his heart, but believes that what he says is happening, he shall have whatever he says. Therefore I tell you, all things whatever you pray and ask for, believe that you have received them, and you shall have them. Whenever you stand praying, forgive, if you have anything against anyone; so that your Father, who is in heaven, may also forgive you your transgressions. But if you do not forgive, neither will your Father in heaven forgive your transgressions" (Mark 11:19-26, also Matthew 21:18-22).

Jesus confronts chief priests and scribes in Temple

They came again to Jerusalem, and as he was walking in the temple, the chief priests, and the scribes, and the elders came to him, and they began saying to him, "By what authority do you do these things? Or who gave you this authority to do these things?"

Jesus said to them, "I will ask you one question. Answer me, and I will tell you by what authority I do these things. The baptism of John—was it from heaven, or from men? Answer me."

They reasoned with themselves, saying, "If we should say, 'From heaven;' he will say, 'Why then did you not believe him?' If we should say, 'From men'"—they feared the people, for all held John to really be a prophet. They answered Jesus, "We don't know."

Jesus said to them, "Neither do I tell you by what authority I do these things" (Mark 11:27-33).

Jesus teaches in parables

[See Lessons: **Parable of Lost Son** (Matthew 21:28b-32), **Parable of the Vineyard** (Matthew 21:33-46, also Mark 12:1-12 and Luke 20:19-26), and **Parable of Feast in God's Kingdom** (Matthew 22:1-14).]

Jesus questioned about taxes

[See Lessons: **Taxes** (Matthew 22:15-22, also Mark 12:13-17, Luke 20:19-26)].

Religious leaders question Jesus about resurrection

When they heard it, they marveled, and left him, and went away.

On that day Sadducees (those who say that there is no resurrection) came to him. They asked him, saying, "Teacher, Moses said, 'If a man dies, having no children, his brother shall marry his wife, and raise up offspring for his brother.' Now there were with us seven brothers. The first married and died, and having no offspring left his wife to his brother. In the same way, the second also, and the third, to the seventh. After them all, the woman died. In the resurrection therefore, whose wife will she be of the seven? For they all had her."

But Jesus answered them, "You are mistaken, not knowing the Scriptures, nor the power of God. For in the resurrection they neither marry, nor are given in marriage, but are like God's angels in heaven. But concerning the resurrection of the dead, haven't you read that which was spoken to you by God, saying, 'I am the God of Abraham, and the God of Isaac, and the God of Jacob?' God is not the God of the dead, but of the living."

When the multitudes heard it, they were astonished at his teaching (Matthew 22:22-23, also Mark 12:18-27, Luke 20:27-40).

Jesus asked what is greatest commandment

But the Pharisees, when they heard that he had silenced the Sadducees, gathered themselves together. One of them, a lawyer, asked him a question, testing him. "Teacher, which is the greatest commandment in the law?"

Jesus said to him, "'You shall love the Lord your God with all your heart, with all your soul, and with all your mind.' This is the first and great commandment. A second likewise is this, 'You shall love your neighbor as yourself.' The whole law and the prophets depend on these two commandments." (Matthew 22:34-40, Mark12: 28-34, Luke 10:25-28).

[See Lessons: **Love**)].

78

Jesus asked who is the Christ

Now while the Pharisees were gathered together, Jesus asked them a question, saying, "What do you think of the Christ? Whose son is he?"

They said to him, "Of David."

He said to them, "How then does David in the Spirit call him Lord, saying,

> 'The Lord said to my Lord,
> sit on my right hand,
> until I make your enemies a footstool for your feet?'

"If then David calls him Lord, how is he his son?"

No one was able to answer him a word, neither did any man dare ask him any more questions from that day forward (Matthew 22:41-46, Mark 12:35-37, Luke 20:41-44).

[See Lessons: **Jesus teaches about himself**.]

Jesus confront the Pharisees

Then Jesus spoke to the multitudes and to his disciples, saying, "The scribes and the Pharisees sat on Moses' seat. All things therefore whatever they tell you to observe, observe and do, but don't do their works; for they say, and don't do" (Matthew 23:1-3)

[See Lessons: **Hypocrisy** (Matthew 23:1-36, Mark 12:38-40, Luke 20:45-47).]

Jesus teaches about abundant giving

He looked up, and saw the rich people who were putting their gifts into the treasury. He saw a certain poor widow casting in two small brass coins. He said, "Truly I tell you, this poor widow put in more than all of them, for all these put in gifts for God from their abundance, but she, out of her poverty, put in all that she had to live on" (Luke 21:1-4, also Mark 12:41-44).

Jesus teaches about end days

As some were talking about the temple and how it was decorated with beautiful stones and gifts, he said, "As for these things which you see, the days will come, in which there will not be left here one stone on another that will not be thrown down."

They asked him, "Teacher, so when will these things be? What is the sign that these things are about to happen?" (Luke 21:5-7, also Matthew 24:1-3, Mark 13:1-4)

[See Lessons: **End days** (Matthew 24:1-25:46, also Mark 13:1-37, Luke 21:8-36).]

Jesus once again predicts his crucifixion

When Jesus had finished all these words, he said to his disciples, "You know that after two days the Passover is coming, and the Son of Man will be delivered up to be crucified."

Then the chief priests, the scribes, and the elders of the people were gathered together in the court of the high priest, who was called Caiaphas. They took counsel together that they might take Jesus by deceit and kill him. But they said, "Not during the feast, lest a riot occur among the people" (Matthew 26:1-5, Luke 22:1-2, John 11:45-53).

Jesus teaches in the Temple

Every day Jesus was teaching in the Temple, and every night he would go out and spend the night on the mountain that is called Olivet. All the people came early in the morning to him in the temple to hear him (Luke 21:37-38).

Jesus again foretells his death

Now there were certain Greeks among those that went up to worship at the feast. These, therefore, came to Philip, who was from Bethsaida of Galilee, and asked him, saying, "Sir, we want to see Jesus." Philip came and told Andrew, and in turn, Andrew came with Philip, and they told Jesus. Jesus answered them, "The time has come for the Son of Man to be glorified. Most certainly I tell you, unless a grain of wheat falls into the earth and dies, it remains by itself alone. But if it dies, it bears much fruit. He who loves his life will lose it. He who hates his life in this world will keep it to eternal life. If anyone serves me, let him follow me. Where I am, there will my servant also be. If anyone serves me, the Father will honor him (John 12:20-26).

God the Father proclaims Jesus is his Son
"Now my soul is troubled. What shall I say? 'Father, save me from this time?' But for this cause I came to this time. Father, glorify your name!"

Then there came a voice out of the sky, saying, "I have both glorified it, and will glorify it again."

The multitude therefore, who stood by and heard it, said that it had thundered. Others said, "An angel has spoken to him."

Jesus answered, "This voice hasn't come for my sake, but for your sakes (John 12:27-30).

Jesus continues teaching in the Temple
Now is the judgment of this world. Now the prince of this world will be cast out. And I, if I am lifted up from the earth, will draw all people to myself." But he said this, signifying by what kind of death he should die. The multitude answered him, "We have heard out of the law that the Christ remains forever. How do you say, 'The Son of Man must be lifted up?' Who is this Son of Man?"

Jesus therefore said to them, "Yet a little while the light is with you. Walk while you have the light, that darkness doesn't overtake you. He who walks in the darkness doesn't know where he is going. While you have the light, believe in the light, that you may become children of light." Jesus said these things, and he departed and hid himself from them. But though he had done so many signs before them, yet they didn't believe in him, that the word of Isaiah the prophet might be fulfilled, which he spoke,

"Lord, who has believed our report?
To whom has the arm of the Lord been revealed?"

For this cause they couldn't believe, for Isaiah said again,

"He has blinded their eyes and he hardened their heart,
lest they should see with their eyes,

81

and perceive with their heart,
and would turn,
and I would heal them."

Isaiah said these things when he saw his glory, and spoke of him. Nevertheless even of the rulers many believed in him, but because of the Pharisees they didn't confess it, so that they wouldn't be put out of the synagogue, for they loved men's praise more than God's praise.

Jesus cried out and said, "Whoever believes in me, believes not in me, but in him who sent me. He who sees me sees him who sent me. I have come as a light into the world, that whoever believes in me may not remain in the darkness. If anyone listens to my sayings, and doesn't believe, I don't judge him. For I came not to judge the world, but to save the world. He who rejects me, and doesn't receive my sayings, has one who judges him. The word that I spoke, the same will judge him in the last day. For I spoke not from myself, but the Father who sent me, he gave me a commandment, what I should say, and what I should speak. I know that his commandment is eternal life. The things therefore which I speak, even as the Father has said to me, so I speak" (John 12:31-50).

Religious leaders and Judas plot to kill Jesus

Now the feast of unleavened bread, which is called the Passover, was approaching. The chief priests and the scribes sought how they might put him to death, for they feared the people. Satan entered into Judas, who was also called Iscariot, who was numbered with the twelve. He went away, and talked with the chief priests and captains about how he might deliver him to them. They were glad, and agreed to give him money. He consented, and sought an opportunity to deliver him to them in the absence of the multitude (Luke 22:1-6, also Matthew 26:1-5, 14-16; Mark 14:10-11; John 11:45-53)

Jesus celebrates Passover with his disciples

The day of unleavened bread came, on which the Passover must be sacrificed. He sent Peter and John, saying, "Go and prepare the Passover for us, that we may eat."

They said to him, "Where do you want us to prepare?"

He said to them, "Behold, when you have entered into the city, a man carrying a pitcher of water will meet you. Follow him into the house which he enters. Tell the master of the house, 'The Teacher says to you, "Where is the guest room, where I may eat the Passover with my disciples?"' He will show you a large, furnished upper room. Make preparations there."

They went, found things as he had told them, and they prepared the Passover. When the hour had come, he sat down with the twelve apostles (Luke 22:7-14).

Jesus washes disciples' feet

Now before the feast of the Passover, Jesus, knowing that his time had come that he would depart from this world to the Father, having loved his own who were in the world, he loved them to the end. During supper, the devil having already put into the heart of Judas Iscariot, Simon's son, to betray him, Jesus, knowing that the Father had given all things into his hands, and that he came from God and was going to God, arose from supper and laid aside his outer garments. He took a towel and wrapped a towel around his waist. Then he poured water into the basin and began to wash the disciples' feet and to wipe them with the towel that was wrapped around him. Then he came to Simon Peter. He said to him, "Lord, do you wash my feet?"

Jesus answered him, "You don't know what I am doing now, but you will understand later."

Peter said to him, "You will never wash my feet!"

Jesus answered him, "If I don't wash you, you have no part with me."

Simon Peter said to him, "Lord, not my feet only, but also my hands and my head!"

Jesus said to him, "Someone who has bathed only needs to have his feet washed, but is completely clean. You are clean, but not all of you." For he knew him who would betray him, therefore he said, "You are not all clean." So when he had washed their feet, put his outer garment back on, and sat down again, he said to them, "Do you know what I have done to you? You call me, 'Teacher' and 'Lord.'

You say so correctly, for so I am. If I then, the Lord and the Teacher, have washed your feet, you also ought to wash one another's feet. For I have given you an example, that you also should do as I have done to you. Most certainly I tell you, a servant is not greater than his lord, neither one who is sent greater than he who sent him. If you know these things, blessed are you if you do them. I don't speak concerning all of you. I know whom I have chosen. But that the Scripture may be fulfilled, 'He who eats bread with me has lifted up his heel against me.' From now on, I tell you before it happens, that when it happens, you may believe that I am he. Most certainly I tell you, he who receives whomever I send, receives me; and he who receives me, receives him who sent me" (John 13:1-20).

Jesus institutes Communion

He said to them, "I have earnestly desired to eat this Passover with you before I suffer, for I tell you, I will no longer by any means eat of it until it is fulfilled in God's Kingdom."

He received a cup, and when he had given thanks, he said, "Take this, and share it among yourselves, for I tell you, I will not drink at all again from the fruit of the vine until God's Kingdom comes."

He took bread, and when he had given thanks, he broke it and gave to them, saying, "This is my body which is given for you. Do this in memory of me." Likewise, he took the cup after supper, saying, "This cup is the new covenant in my blood, which is poured out for you" (Luke 22:17-20).

Jesus predicts his betrayal

"But behold, the hand of him who betrays me is with me on the table. The Son of Man indeed goes, as it has been determined, but woe to that man through whom he is betrayed!"

They began to question among themselves, which of them it was who would do this thing (Luke 22:21-23).

One of his disciples, whom Jesus loved, was at the table, leaning against Jesus' breast. Simon Peter therefore beckoned to him and said to him, "Tell us who it is of whom he speaks."

He, leaning back on Jesus' breast, asked him, "Lord, who is it?"

Jesus therefore answered, "It is he to whom I will give this piece of bread when I have dipped it." So when he had dipped the piece of bread, he gave it to Judas, the son of Simon Iscariot. After the piece of bread, then Satan entered into him.

Then Jesus said to him, "What you do, do quickly."

Now no man at the table knew why he said this to him. For some thought, because Judas had the money box, that Jesus said to him, "Buy what things we need for the feast," or that he should give something to the poor. Therefore having received that morsel, he went out immediately. It was night (John 13:23-30).

Jesus declares a new commandment

When [Judas] had gone out, Jesus said, "Now the Son of Man has been glorified, and God has been glorified in him. If God has been glorified in him, God will also glorify him in himself, and he will glorify him immediately. Little children, I will be with you a little while longer. You will seek me, and as I said to the Jews, 'Where I am going, you can't come,' so now I tell you. A new commandment I give to you, that you love one another. Just as I have loved you, you also love one another. By this everyone will know that you are my disciples, if you have love for one another" (John 13:31-35).

Disciples argue who is the greatest

There arose also a contention among [the disciples], which of them was considered to be greatest. [Jesus] said to them, "The kings of the nations lord it over them, and those who have authority over them are called 'benefactors.' But not so with you. But one who is the greater among you, let him become as the younger, and one who is governing, as one who serves. For who is greater, one who sits at the table or one who serves? Isn't it he who sits at the table? But I am among you as one who serves. But you are those who have continued with me in my trials. I confer on you a kingdom, even as my Father conferred on me, that you may eat and drink at my table in my Kingdom. You will sit on thrones, judging the twelve tribes of Israel." (Luke 22:24-30).

Jesus predicts disciples denial, desertion

Jesus said to them, "All of you will be made to stumble because of me tonight, for it is written, 'I will strike the shepherd, and the sheep will be scattered.' However, after I am raised up, I will go before you into Galilee."

But Peter said to him, "Although all will be offended, yet I will not" (Mark 14:27-29, also Matthew 26:31-35, John 13:36-38).

The Lord said, "Simon, Simon, behold, Satan asked to have you, that he might sift you as wheat, but I prayed for you, that your faith wouldn't fail. You, when once you have turned again, establish your brothers."

He said to him, "Lord, I am ready to go with you both to prison and to death!"

He said, "I tell you, Peter, the rooster will by no means crow today until you deny that you know me three times."

He said to them, "When I sent you out without purse, wallet, and shoes, did you lack anything?"

They said, "Nothing."

Then he said to them, "But now, whoever has a purse, let him take it, and likewise a wallet. Whoever has none, let him sell his cloak and buy a sword. For I tell you that this which is written must still be fulfilled in me: 'He was counted with transgressors.' For that which concerns me has an end."

They said, "Lord, behold, here are two swords."

He said to them, "That is enough" (Luke 22:31-38).

Jesus assures his disciples of eternal life

[See Lessons: **Eternal life** (John 14:1-7).]

Jesus assures disciples he and Father are one

Thomas said to him, "Lord, we don't know where you are going. How can we know the way?"

Jesus said to him, "I am the way, the truth, and the life. No one comes to the Father, except through me. If you had known me, you would have known my Father also. From now on, you know him, and have seen him."

Philip said to him, "Lord, show us the Father, and that will be enough for us" (John 14:5-8).

[See Lessons: **Jesus teaches about himself** (John 14:9-21).]

Jesus answers additional questions
[See Lessons: **Holy Spirit, Obedience** (John 14:22-31).]

Jesus' final teaching in the Garden of Gethsemane
[See Lessons: **Fruit** (John 15:1-7), **Holy Spirit** (John 15:26-27, 16:7-16), **Love** (John 15:8-17), **Persecution** (John 15:18-25, 16:1-6).]

Some of his disciples therefore said to one another, "What is this that he says to us, 'A little while, and you won't see me, and again a little while, and you will see me;' and, 'Because I go to the Father'?" They said therefore, "What is this that he says, 'A little while'? We don't know what he is saying."

Therefore Jesus perceived that they wanted to ask him, and he said to them, "Do you inquire among yourselves concerning this, that I said, 'A little while, and you won't see me, and again a little while, and you will see me?' Most certainly I tell you, that you will weep and lament, but the world will rejoice. You will be sorrowful, but your sorrow will be turned into joy. A woman, when she gives birth, has sorrow, because her time has come. But when she has delivered the child, she doesn't remember the anguish any more, for the joy that a human being is born into the world. Therefore you now have sorrow, but I will see you again, and your heart will rejoice, and no one will take your joy away from you.

"In that day you will ask me no questions (John 16:17-23a).

[See Lessons: **Prayer** John 16:23b-28)].

His disciples said to him, "Behold, now you speak plainly, and speak no figures of speech. Now we know that you know all things, and don't need for anyone to question you. By this we believe that you came from God."

Jesus answered them, "Do you now believe? Behold, the time is coming, yes, and has now come, that you will be scattered, everyone to his own place, and you will leave me alone. Yet I am not alone, because the Father is with me. I have told you these things, that in me you may have peace. In the world you have oppression; but cheer up! I have overcome the world" (John 16:29-33).

Jesus prays for present, future disciples

Jesus said these things, and lifting up his eyes to heaven, he said, "Father, the time has come. Glorify your Son, that your Son may also glorify you; even as you gave him authority over all flesh, he will give eternal life to all whom you have given him. This is eternal life, that they should know you, the only true God, and him whom you sent, Jesus Christ. I glorified you on the earth. I have accomplished the work which you have given me to do. Now, Father, glorify me with your own self with the glory which I had with you before the world existed. I revealed your name to the people whom you have given me out of the world. They were yours, and you have given them to me. They have kept your word. Now they have known that all things whatever you have given me are from you, for the words which you have given me I have given to them, and they received them, and knew for sure that I came from you, and they have believed that you sent me. I pray for them. I don't pray for the world, but for those whom you have given me, for they are yours. All things that are mine are yours, and yours are mine, and I am glorified in them. I am no more in the world, but these are in the world, and I am coming to you. Holy Father, keep them through your name which you have given me, that they may be one, even as we are. While I was with them in the world, I kept them in your name. Those whom you have given me I have kept. None of them is lost, except the son of destruction, that the Scripture might be fulfilled. But now I come to you, and I say these things in the world, that they may have my joy made full in themselves. I have given them your word. The world hated them, because they are not of the world, even as I am not of the world. I pray not that you would take them from the world, but that you would keep them from the evil one. They are not of the world even as I am not of the world.

Sanctify them in your truth. Your word is truth. As you sent me into the world, even so I have sent them into the world. For their sakes I sanctify myself, that they themselves also may be sanctified in truth. Not for these only do I pray, but for those also who believe in me through their word, that they may all be one; even as you, Father, are in me, and I in you, that they also may be one in us; that the world may believe that you sent me. The glory which you have given me, I have given to them; that they may be one, even as we are one; I in them, and you in me, that they may be perfected into one; that the world may know that you sent me, and loved them, even as you loved me. Father, I desire that they also whom you have given me be with me where I am, that they may see my glory, which you have given me, for you loved me before the foundation of the world. Righteous Father, the world hasn't known you, but I knew you; and these knew that you sent me. I made known to them your name, and will make it known; that the love with which you loved me may be in them, and I in them" (John 17:1-26).

Jesus asks disciples to pray with him

Then Jesus . . . said to his disciples, "Sit here, while I go there and pray." He took with him Peter and the two sons of Zebedee and began to be sorrowful and severely troubled. Then he said to them, "My soul is exceedingly sorrowful, even to death. Stay here, and watch with me."

He went forward a little, fell on his face, and prayed, saying, "My Father, if it is possible, let this cup pass away from me; nevertheless, not what I desire, but what you desire."

He came to the disciples, and found them sleeping, and said to Peter, "What, couldn't you watch with me for one hour? Watch and pray, that you don't enter into temptation. The spirit indeed is willing, but the flesh is weak."

Again, a second time he went away, and prayed, saying, "My Father, if this cup can't pass away from me unless I drink it, your desire be done." He came again and found them sleeping, for their eyes were heavy. He left them again, went away, and prayed a third time, saying the same words. Then he came to his disciples, and said to them, "Sleep on now, and take your rest. Behold, the hour is at hand, and the Son of Man is betrayed into the hands of sinners. Arise, let's be going. Behold, he who betrays me is at hand" (Matthew 26:36-46, also Mark 14:26, 32-42, Luke 22:39-46).

Mob arrests Jesus

While he was still speaking, behold, Judas, one of the twelve, came and with him a great multitude with swords and clubs from the chief priest and elders of the people. Now he who betrayed him gave them a sign, saying, "Whoever I kiss, he is the one. Seize him" (Matthew 26:47-48, also Mark 14:43-50, Luke 22:47-53, John 18:3-12).

Jesus therefore, knowing all the things that were happening to him, went out, and said to them, "Who are you looking for?"

They answered him, "Jesus of Nazareth."

Jesus said to them, "I am he." Judas also, who betrayed him, was standing with them. When therefore he said to them, "I am he," they went backward, and fell to the ground.

Again therefore he asked them, "Who are you looking for?"

They said, "Jesus of Nazareth" (John 18:4-7).

[Judas] came near to Jesus to kiss him. But Jesus said to him, "Judas, do you betray the Son of Man with a kiss?" (Luke 22:47b-48, also Mark 14:45).

Then they came and laid hands on Jesus, and took him (Matthew 26:50b, also Mark 14:46).

Simon Peter therefore, having a sword, drew it, and struck the high priest's servant and cut off his right ear. The servant's name was Malchus (John 18:10-11, also Matthew 26:51, Mark 14:47, Luke 22:50).

Then Jesus said to him, "Put your sword back into its place, for all those who take the sword will die by the sword. Or do you think that I couldn't ask my Father, and he would even now send me more than twelve legions of angels?" (Matthew 26:52-53).

[Jesus] touched [the servant's] ear and healed him.

Jesus said to the chief priests, captains of the temple, and elders who had come against him, "Have you come out as against a robber, with swords and clubs? When I was with you in the temple daily, you didn't stretch out your hands against me. But this is your hour and the power of darkness" (Luke 22:51-53, also Mark 14:48-49).

But all this has happened, that the Scriptures of the prophets might be fulfilled" (Matthew 26:56).

[The disciples] all left him, and fled. A certain young man followed him, having a linen cloth thrown around himself, over his naked body. [A member of the mob] grabbed him, but he left the linen cloth and fled from them naked (Mark 14:50-52).

Jesus brought before Annas, the former chief priest

So the detachment, the commanding officer, and the officers of the Jews seized Jesus and bound him and led him to Annas first, for he was father-in-law to Caiaphas, who was high priest that year. Now it was Caiaphas who advised the Jews that it was expedient that one man should perish for the people (John 18:12-14, Matthew 26:57-58, Mark 14:53, Luke 22:54).

Peter had followed [Jesus] from a distance, until he came into the court of the high priest. He was sitting with the officers, and warming himself in the light of the fire (Mark 14:54).

[Annas] therefore asked Jesus about his disciples, and about his teaching. Jesus answered him, "I spoke openly to the world. I always taught in synagogues and in the temple, where the Jews always meet. I said nothing in secret. Why do you ask me? Ask those who have heard me what I said to them. Behold, these know the things which I said."

When he had said this, one of the officers standing by slapped Jesus with his hand saying, "Do you answer the high priest like that?"

Jesus answered him, "If I have spoken evil, testify of the evil; but if well, why do you beat me?" Annas sent him bound to Caiaphas, the high priest. (John 18:19-23, Matthew 26:59-66, Mark 14:55).

False witnesses sought to testify against Jesus

Now the chief priests and the whole council sought witnesses against Jesus to put him to death and found none. For many gave false testimony against him, and their testimony didn't agree with each other. Some stood up and gave false testimony against him saying, "We heard him say, 'I will destroy this temple that is made with hands, and in three days I will build another made without hands.'" Even so, their testimony did not agree (Mark 14:56-59, also Matthew 26:59-61).

Caiaphas, the high priest, condemns Jesus

The high priest stood up in the middle and asked Jesus, "Have you no answer? What is it which these testify against you?" But he stayed quiet, and answered nothing. Again the high priest asked him, "Are you the Christ, the Son of the Blessed?"

Jesus said, "I am. You will see the Son of Man sitting at the right hand of Power and coming with the clouds of the sky."

The high priest tore his clothes and said, "What further need have we of witnesses? You have heard the blasphemy! What do you think?" They all condemned him to be worthy of death (Mark 14:60-64, also Matthew 26:62-66, Luke 22:66-71).

Members of Sanhedrin beat Jesus

Some began to spit on him, and to cover his face, and to beat him with fists, and to tell him, "Prophesy!" The officers struck him with the palms of their hands (Mark 14:65, also Matthew 26:67-68, Luke 22:63-65).

Peter denies Jesus first time

As Peter was in the courtyard below, one of the maids of the high priest came and seeing Peter warming himself, she looked at him, and said, "You were also with the Nazarene, Jesus!"

But he denied it, saying, "I neither know, nor understand what you are saying." He went out on the porch, and the rooster crowed (Mark 14:66-68, also Matthew 26:69-70, Luke 22:55-57, John 18:17-18).

Peter denies Jesus second and third times

The maid . . . began . . . to tell those who stood by, "This is one of them." But he again denied it. After a little while again those who stood by said to Peter, "You truly are one of them, for you are a Galilean, and your speech shows it" (Mark 14:69-70, also Matthew 26:69-73, Luke 22:58-59).

One of the servants of the high priest, being a relative of him whose ear Peter had cut off, said, "Didn't I see you in the garden with him?" (John 18:26).

But Peter said, "Man, I don't know what you are talking about!" Immediately, while he was still speaking, a rooster crowed. The Lord turned, and looked at Peter. Then Peter remembered the Lord's word, how he said to him, "Before the rooster crows you will deny me three times." He went out, and wept bitterly (Luke 22:60-62, also Mark 14:71-72, also Matthew 26:73-74).

Judas regrets betraying Jesus, hangs himself

Then Judas, who betrayed him, when he saw that Jesus was condemned, felt remorse and brought back the thirty pieces of silver to the chief priests and elders, saying, "I have sinned in that I betrayed innocent blood."

But they said, "What is that to us? You see to it."

He threw down the pieces of silver in the sanctuary and departed. He went away and hanged himself. The chief priests took the pieces of silver and said, "It's not lawful to put them into the treasury, since it is the price of blood." They took counsel, and bought the potter's field with them, to bury strangers in. Therefore that field was called "The Field of Blood" to this day. Then that which was spoken through Jeremiah the prophet was fulfilled, saying,

"They took the thirty pieces of silver,
the price of him upon whom a price had been set,
whom some of the children of Israel priced,
and they gave them for the potter's field,
as the Lord commanded me" (Matthew 27:3-10)

Christ appears before Pilate

[The religious leaders] led Jesus therefore from Caiaphas into the Praetorium. It was early, and they themselves didn't enter into the Praetorium, that they might not be defiled, but might eat the Passover. Pilate therefore went out to them, and said, "What accusation do you bring against this man?"

They answered him, "If this man weren't an evildoer, we wouldn't have delivered him up to you."

Pilate therefore said to them, "Take him yourselves, and judge him according to your law."

Therefore the Jews said to him, "It is not lawful for us to put anyone to death," that the word of Jesus might be fulfilled, which he spoke, signifying by what kind of death he should die.

Pilate therefore entered again into the Praetorium, called Jesus, and said to him, "Are you the King of the Jews?"

Jesus answered him, "Do you say this by yourself, or did others tell you about me?"

Pilate answered, "I'm not a Jew, am I? Your own nation and the chief priests delivered you to me. What have you done?"

Jesus answered, "My Kingdom is not of this world. If my Kingdom were of this world, then my servants would fight, that I wouldn't be delivered to the Jews. But now my Kingdom is not from here."

Pilate therefore said to him, "Are you a king then?"

Jesus answered, "You say that I am a king. For this reason I have been born, and for this reason I have come into the world, that I should testify to the truth. Everyone who is of the truth listens to my voice."

Pilate said to him, "What is truth?"

When he had said this, he went out again to the Jews, and said to them, "I find no basis for a charge against him (John 18:28-38; also Matthew 27:1-2, Mark 15:1-2, Luke 23:1-5).

When he was accused by the chief priests and elders, he answered nothing. Then Pilate said to him, "Don't you hear how many things they testify against you?"

He gave him no answer, not even one word, so that the governor marveled greatly (Matthew 27:12-14, Mark 15:3-5).

Pilate sends Jesus to Herod

But they insisted, saying, "He stirs up the people, teaching throughout all Judea, beginning from Galilee even to this place." But when Pilate heard Galilee mentioned, he asked if the man was a Galilean. When he found out that he was in Herod's jurisdiction, he sent him to Herod, who was also in Jerusalem during those days.

Now when Herod saw Jesus, he was exceedingly glad, for he had wanted to see him for a long time, because he had heard many things about him. He hoped to see some miracle done by him. He questioned him with many words, but he gave no answers. The chief priests and the scribes stood, vehemently accusing him. Herod with his soldiers humiliated him and mocked him. Dressing him in luxurious clothing, they sent him back to Pilate. Herod and Pilate became friends with each other that very day, for before that they were enemies with each other.

Pilate called together the chief priests and the rulers and the people, and said to them, "You brought this man to me as one that perverts the people, and see, I have examined him before you, and found no basis for a charge against this man concerning those things of which you accuse him. Neither has Herod, for I sent you to him, and see, nothing worthy of death has been done by him. (Luke 23:5-15).

Jesus appears before Pilate a second time

Now at the feast he used to release to them one prisoner, whom they asked of him. There was one called Barabbas, bound with his fellow insurgents, men who in the insurrection had committed murder. The multitude, crying aloud, began to ask him to do as he always did for them. Pilate answered them, saying, "Do you want me to release to you the King of the Jews?" For he perceived that for envy the chief priests had delivered him up (Mark 15:6-10, also Matthew 27:15-18, John 18:30).

While he was sitting on the judgment seat, his wife sent to him, saying, "Have nothing to do with that righteous man, for I have suffered many things today in a dream because of him." Now the chief priests and the elders persuaded the multitudes to ask for Barabbas, and destroy Jesus. (Matthew 27:19-20).

But they all cried out together, saying, "Away with this man! Release to us Barabbas!"—one who was thrown into prison for a certain revolt in the city, and for murder (Luke 23:18-19, also John 18:40).

So Pilate then took Jesus, and flogged him. The soldiers twisted thorns into a crown, and put it on his head, and dressed him in a purple garment. They kept saying, "Hail, King of the Jews!" and they kept slapping him.

Then Pilate went out again, and said to them, "Behold, I bring him out to you, that you may know that I find no basis for a charge against him."

Jesus therefore came out, wearing the crown of thorns and the purple garment. Pilate said to them, "Behold, the man!"

When therefore the chief priests and the officers saw him, they shouted, saying, "Crucify! Crucify!"

Pilate said to them, "Take him yourselves, and crucify him, for I find no basis for a charge against him."

The Jews answered him, "We have a law, and by our law he ought to die, because he made himself the Son of God."

When therefore Pilate heard this saying, he was more afraid. He entered into the Praetorium again, and said to Jesus, "Where are you from?" But Jesus gave him no answer. Pilate therefore said to him, "Aren't you speaking to me? Don't you know that I have power to release you, and have power to crucify you?"

Jesus answered, "You would have no power at all against me, unless it were given to you from above. Therefore he who delivered me to you has greater sin."

At this, Pilate was seeking to release him, but the Jews cried out, saying, "If you release this man, you aren't Caesar's friend! Everyone who makes himself a king speaks against Caesar!"

When Pilate therefore heard these words, he brought Jesus out, and sat down on the judgment seat at a place called "The Pavement", but in Hebrew, "Gabbatha." Now it was the Preparation Day of the Passover, at about the sixth hour. He said to the Jews, "Behold, your King!"

They cried out, "Away with him! Away with him! Crucify him!"

Pilate said to them, "Shall I crucify your King?"

The chief priests answered, "We have no king but Caesar!" (John 19:1-15, also Matthew 27:22-23, Mark 15:12-14, Luke 23:20-22).

So when Pilate saw that nothing was being gained, but rather that a disturbance was starting, he took water, and washed his hands before the multitude, saying, "I am innocent of the blood of this righteous person. You see to it."

All the people answered, "May his blood be on us, and on our children!" (Matthew 27:24-25).

Pilate condemns Jesus to be crucified

Pilate decreed that what they asked for should be done. He released him who had been thrown into prison for insurrection and murder, for whom they asked, but he delivered Jesus up to their will (Luke 23:24-25, also Matthew 27:26, Mark 15:15).

Then the governor's soldiers took Jesus into the Praetorium, and gathered the whole garrison together against him. They stripped him, and put a scarlet robe on him. They braided a crown of thorns and put it on his head, and a reed in his right hand; and they kneeled down before him, and mocked him, saying, "Hail, King of the Jews!" They spat on him, and took the reed and struck him on the head. When they had mocked him, they took the robe off of him, and put his clothes on him, and led him away to crucify him (Matthew 27:27-31, also Mark 15:16-19).

Jesus led to cross
[Jesus] went out, bearing his cross, [toward] the place called "The Place of a Skull," which is called in Hebrew, "Golgotha" (John 19:16-17, also Matthew 27:31, Mark 15:20).

They compelled one passing by, coming from the country, Simon of Cyrene, the father of Alexander and Rufus, to go with them, that he might bear his cross (Mark 15:21, also Matthew 27:32, Luke 23:26).

A great multitude including women following Jesus to cross
A great multitude of the people followed him, including women who also mourned and lamented him. But Jesus, turning to them, said, "Daughters of Jerusalem, don't weep for me, but weep for yourselves and for your children. For behold, the days are coming in which they will say, 'Blessed are the barren, the wombs that never bore, and the breasts that never nursed.' Then they will begin to tell the mountains, 'Fall on us!' and tell the hills, 'Cover us.' For if they do these things in the green tree, what will be done in the dry?" (Luke 23:27-31).

Jesus crucified
They offered him wine mixed with myrrh to drink, but he didn't take it (Mark 15:23, Matthew 27:34).

It was [9 A.M.], and they crucified him (Mark 15:25).

Then the soldiers, when they had crucified Jesus, took his garments and made four parts, to every soldier a part; and also the coat. Now the coat was without seam, woven from the top throughout. Then they said to one another, "Let's not tear it, but cast lots for it to decide whose it will be," that the Scripture might be fulfilled, which says,

"They parted my garments among them.
For my cloak they cast lots."
Therefore the soldiers did these things. (John 19:23-24,
also Matthew 27:35, Mark 15:24, Luke 23:34b).

Pilate wrote a title also, and put it on the cross. There was written, "JESUS OF NAZARETH, THE KING OF THE JEWS." Therefore many of the Jews read this title, for the place where Jesus was crucified was near the city; and it was written in Hebrew, in Latin, and in Greek. The chief priests of the Jews therefore said to Pilate, "Don't write, 'The King of the Jews,' but, 'he said, I am King of the Jews.'"

Pilate answered, "What I have written, I have written" (John 19:19-22, also Matthew 27:37, Mark 15:26, Luke 23:38).

There were also others, two criminals, led with him to be put to death . . . one on the right and the other on the left (Luke 23:32-33, also Matthew 27:38, Mark 15:27, John 19:18).

One of the criminals who was hanged insulted him, saying, "If you are the Christ, save yourself and us!"

But the other answered, and rebuking him said, "Don't you even fear God, seeing you are under the same condemnation? And we indeed justly, for we receive the due reward for our deeds, but this man has done nothing wrong." He said to Jesus, "Lord, remember me when you come into your Kingdom."

Jesus said to him, "Assuredly I tell you, today you will be with me in Paradise" (Luke 23:39-43).

Those who passed by blasphemed him, wagging their heads, and saying, "You who destroy the temple, and build it in three days, save yourself! If you are the Son of God, come down from the cross!"

Likewise the chief priests also mocking, with the scribes, the Pharisees, and the elders, said, "He saved others, but he can't save himself. If he is the King of Israel, let him come down from the cross now, and we will believe in him. He trusts in God. Let God deliver him now, if he wants him; for he said, 'I am the Son of God'" (Matthew 27:39-43, also Mark 15:29-32, Luke 23:35-36,).

Jesus said, "Father, forgive them, for they don't know what they are doing" (Luke 23:34).

There were standing by the cross of Jesus his mother, and his mother's sister, Mary the wife of Clopas, and Mary Magdalene. Therefore when Jesus saw his mother, and the disciple whom he loved standing there, he said to his mother, "Woman, behold your son!" Then he said to the disciple, "Behold, your mother!" From that hour, the disciple took her to his own home (John 19:25-27)

When the [noon] hour had come, there was darkness over the whole land until [3 P.M.]. At [that time], Jesus cried with a loud voice, saying, *"Eloi, Eloi, lama sabachthani?"* which is, being interpreted, "My God, my God, why have you forsaken me?"
Some of those who stood by, when they heard it, said, "Behold, he is calling Elijah" (Mark 15:33-35, also Matthew 27:45-47, Luke 23:44-45).

After this, Jesus, seeing that all things were now finished, that the Scripture might be fulfilled, said, "I am thirsty." Now a vessel full of vinegar was set there; so they put a sponge full of the vinegar on hyssop, and held it at his mouth (John 19:28-29, also Matthew 27: 48, Mark 15:36,).

The rest said, "Let him be. Let's see whether Elijah comes to save him." (Matthew 27:49).

Jesus, crying with a loud voice, said, "Father, into your hands I commit my spirit!" Having said this, he breathed his last (Luke 23:46).
[John 19:30 records Jesus also saying, "It is finished!"]

Behold, the veil of the temple was torn in two from the top to the bottom. The earth quaked and the rocks were split. The tombs were opened, and many bodies of the saints who had fallen asleep were raised; and coming out of the tombs after his resurrection, they entered into the holy city and appeared to many. Now the centurion, and those who were with him watching Jesus, when they saw the earthquake, and the things that were done, feared exceedingly, saying, "Truly this was the Son of God" (Matthew 27:51-54, also Mark 15:38-39, Luke 23:45-47).

All the multitudes that came together to see this, when they saw the things that were done, returned home beating their breasts. All his acquaintances, and the women who followed with him from Galilee, stood at a distance, watching these things (Luke 23:48-49).

There were also women watching from afar, among whom were both Mary Magdalene, and Mary the mother of James the less and of Joses, and Salome; who, when he was in Galilee, followed him, and served him; and many other women who came up with him to Jerusalem (Mark 15:40-41).

Therefore the Jews, because it was the Preparation Day, so that the bodies wouldn't remain on the cross on the Sabbath (for that Sabbath was a special one), asked of Pilate that their legs might be broken, and that they might be taken away. Therefore the soldiers came, and broke the legs of the first, and of the other who was crucified with him; but when they came to Jesus, and saw that he was already dead, they didn't break his legs. However one of the soldiers pierced his side with a spear, and immediately blood and water came out. He who has seen has testified, and his testimony is true. He knows that he tells the truth, that you may believe. For these things happened, that the Scripture might be fulfilled, "A bone of him will not be broken." Again another Scripture says, "They will look on him whom they pierced" (John 19-31-37).

Jesus is buried in nearby tomb

When evening had now come, because it was the Preparation Day, that is, the day before the Sabbath, Joseph of Arimathaea, a prominent council member who also himself was looking for God's

Kingdom, came. He boldly went in to Pilate, and asked for Jesus' body. Pilate marveled if he were already dead; and summoning the centurion, he asked him whether he had been dead long. When he found out from the centurion, he granted the body to Joseph (Mark 15:42-45, also Matthew 27:57-58, Luke 23:50-52, John 19:38).

He came therefore and took away his body. Nicodemus, who at first came to Jesus by night, also came bringing a mixture of myrrh and aloes, about [seventy-two] pounds. So they took Jesus' body, and bound it in linen cloths with the spices, as the custom of the Jews is to bury. Now in the place where he was crucified there was a garden. In the garden was a new tomb in which no man had ever yet been laid. Then because of the Jews' Preparation Day (for the tomb was near at hand) they laid Jesus there (John 19:38b-42, also Matthew 27:59-60, Mark 15:46, Luke 23:53-54).

The women . . . followed after, and saw the tomb, and how his body was laid. They returned, and prepared spices and ointments. On the Sabbath they rested according to the commandment (Luke 23:55-56).

Now . . . the chief priests and the Pharisees were gathered together to Pilate, saying, "Sir, we remember what that deceiver said while he was still alive: 'After three days I will rise again.' Command therefore that the tomb be made secure until the third day, lest perhaps his disciples come at night and steal him away, and tell the people, 'He is risen from the dead;' and the last deception will be worse than the first."

Pilate said to them, "You have a guard. Go, make it as secure as you can." So they went with the guard and made the tomb secure, sealing the stone (Matthew 27:62-66).

Jesus rises risen from dead

Now after the Sabbath, as it began to dawn on the first day of the week, Mary Magdalene and the other Mary came to see the tomb. Behold, there was a great earthquake, for an angel of the Lord descended from the sky, and came and rolled away the stone from the door, and sat on it. His appearance was like lightning, and his clothing white as snow. For fear of him, the guards shook, and became like dead men (Matthew 28:1-4, also Mark 16:1).

Entering into the tomb, [the women] saw a young man sitting on the right side, dressed in a white robe, and they were amazed. He said to them, "Don't be amazed. You seek Jesus, the Nazarene, who has been crucified. He has risen. He is not here. Behold, the place where they laid him! But go, tell his disciples and Peter, 'He goes before you into Galilee. There you will see him, as he said to you.'"

They went out, and fled from the tomb, for trembling and astonishment had come on them (Mark 16:5-8a, also Luke 24:1-8, John 20:1).

[Mary Magdalene] ran and came to Simon Peter, and to the other disciple whom Jesus loved, and said to them, "They have taken away the Lord out of the tomb, and we don't know where they have laid him!"

Therefore Peter and the other disciple went out, and they went toward the tomb. They both ran together. The other disciple outran Peter, and came to the tomb first. Stooping and looking in, he saw the linen cloths lying, yet he didn't enter in. Then Simon Peter came, following him, and entered into the tomb. He saw the linen cloths lying, and the cloth that had been on his head, not lying with the linen cloths, but rolled up in a place by itself. So then the other disciple who came first to the tomb also entered in, and he saw and believed. For as yet they didn't know the Scripture, that he must rise from the dead. So the disciples went away again to their own homes (John 20:2-10).

Jesus appears to Mary Magdalene

But Mary was standing outside at the tomb weeping. So, as she wept, she stooped and looked into the tomb, and she saw two angels in white sitting, one at the head, and one at the feet, where the body of Jesus had lain. They told her, "Woman, why are you weeping?"

She said to them, "Because they have taken away my Lord, and I don't know where they have laid him." When she had said this, she turned around and saw Jesus standing, and didn't know that it was Jesus.

Jesus said to her, "Woman, why are you weeping? Who are you looking for?"

She, supposing him to be the gardener, said to him, "Sir, if you have carried him away, tell me where you have laid him, and I will take him away."

Jesus said to her, "Mary."

She turned and said to him, "*Rabboni*!" which is to say, "Teacher!"

Jesus said to her, "Don't hold me, for I haven't yet ascended to my Father; but go to my brothers, and tell them, 'I am ascending to my Father and your Father, to my God and your God.'"

Mary Magdalene came and told the disciples that she had seen the Lord, and that he had said these things to her (John 20:11-18, also Mark 16:9-11).

Guards spread rumor that disciples stole Jesus' body

Behold, some of the guards came into the city, and told the chief priests all the things that had happened. When they were assembled with the elders, and had taken counsel, they gave a large amount of silver to the soldiers, saying, "Say that his disciples came by night, and stole him away while we slept. If this comes to the governor's ears, we will persuade him and make you free of worry." So they took the money and did as they were told. This saying was spread abroad among the Jews, and continues until today (Matthew 28:11-15).

Jesus appears to two disciples on road to Emmaus

Behold, two of them were going that very day to a village named Emmaus, which was [seven miles] from Jerusalem. They talked with each other about all of these things which had happened. While they talked and questioned together, Jesus himself came near, and went with them. But their eyes were kept from recognizing him. He said to them, "What are you talking about as you walk, and are sad?"

One of them, named Cleopas, answered him, "Are you the only stranger in Jerusalem who doesn't know the things which have happened there in these days?"

He said to them, "What things?"

They said to him, "The things concerning Jesus, the Nazarene, who was a prophet mighty in deed and word before God and all the people; and how the chief priests and our rulers delivered him up to be condemned to death, and crucified him. But we were hoping that it was he who would redeem Israel. Yes, and besides all this, it is now the third day since these things happened. Also, certain women of our company amazed us, having arrived early at the tomb; and when they didn't find his body, they came saying that they had also seen a vision of angels, who said that he was alive. Some of us went to the tomb, and found it just like the women had said, but they didn't see him."

He said to them, "Foolish men, and slow of heart to believe in all that the prophets have spoken! Didn't the Christ have to suffer these things and to enter into his glory?" Beginning from Moses and from all the prophets, he explained to them in all the Scriptures the things concerning himself. They came near to the village, where they were going, and he acted like he would go further.

They urged him, saying, "Stay with us, for it is almost evening, and the day is almost over."

He went in to stay with them. When he had sat down at the table with them, he took the bread and gave thanks. Breaking it, he gave to them. Their eyes were opened, and they recognized him, and he vanished out of their sight. They said to one another, "Weren't our hearts burning within us, while he spoke to us along the way, and while he opened the Scriptures to us?" (Luke 24:13-32).

Jesus appears to the disciples in Jerusalem

They rose up that very hour, returned to Jerusalem, and found the [disciples] gathered together, and those who were with them, saying, "The Lord is risen indeed, and has appeared to Simon!" They related the things that happened along the way, and how he was recognized by them in the breaking of the bread.

As they said these things, Jesus himself stood among them, and said to them, "Peace be to you."

But they were terrified and filled with fear, and supposed that they had seen a spirit.

He said to them, "Why are you troubled? Why do doubts arise in your hearts? See my hands and my feet, that it is truly me. Touch me and see, for a spirit doesn't have flesh and bones, as you see that I have." When he had said this, he showed them his hands and his feet. While they still didn't believe for joy, and wondered, he said to them, "Do you have anything here to eat?"

They gave him a piece of a broiled fish and some honeycomb. He took them, and ate in front of them (Luke 24:33-43, Mark 16:14, John 20:19-23).

Jesus therefore said to them again, "Peace be to you. As the Father has sent me, even so I send you." When he had said this, he breathed on them, and said to them, "Receive the Holy Spirit! If you forgive anyone's sins, they have been forgiven them. If you retain anyone's sins, they have been retained."

But Thomas, one of the twelve, called Didymus, wasn't with them when Jesus came. The other disciples therefore said to him, "We have seen the Lord!"

But he said to them, "Unless I see in his hands the print of the nails, and put my hand into his side, I will not believe" (John 20:21-25).

Jesus appears again to the disciples

After eight days, again his disciples were inside, and Thomas was with them. Jesus came, the doors being locked, and stood in the middle, and said, "Peace be to you." Then he said to Thomas, "Reach here your finger, and see my hands. Reach here your hand, and put it into my side. Don't be unbelieving, but believing."

Thomas answered him, "My Lord and my God!"

Jesus said to him, "Because you have seen me, you have believed. Blessed are those who have not seen, and have believed."

Therefore Jesus did many other signs in the presence of his disciples, which are not written in this book; but these are written, that you may believe that Jesus is the Christ, the Son of God, and that believing you may have life in his name (John 20:26-31).

Jesus appears to disciples at Sea of Tiberius

After these things, Jesus revealed himself again to the disciples at the sea of Tiberias. He revealed himself this way. Simon Peter, Thomas called Didymus, Nathanael of Cana in Galilee, and the sons of Zebedee, and two others of his disciples were together. Simon Peter said to them, "I'm going fishing."

They told him, "We are also coming with you." They immediately went out, and entered into the boat. That night, they caught nothing. But when day had already come, Jesus stood on the beach, yet the disciples didn't know that it was Jesus. Jesus therefore said to them, "Children, have you anything to eat?"

They answered him, "No."

He said to them, "Cast the net on the right side of the boat, and you will find some."

They cast it therefore, and now they weren't able to draw it in for the multitude of fish. That disciple therefore whom Jesus loved said to Peter, "It's the Lord!"

So when Simon Peter heard that it was the Lord, he wrapped his coat around him (for he was naked), and threw himself into the sea. But the other disciples came in the little boat (for they were not far from the land, but about [one hundred yards] away), dragging the net full of fish. So when they got out on the land, they saw a fire of coals there, and fish laid on it, and bread. Jesus said to them, "Bring some of the fish which you have just caught."

Simon Peter went up, and drew the net to land, full of great fish, one hundred fifty-three; and even though there were so many, the net wasn't torn.

Jesus said to them, "Come and eat breakfast."

None of the disciples dared inquire of him, "Who are you?" knowing that it was the Lord.

Then Jesus came and took the bread, gave it to them, and the fish likewise. This is now the third time that Jesus was revealed to his disciples, after he had risen from the dead (John 21:2-14).

Jesus reconfirms Peter's commission

So when they had eaten their breakfast, Jesus said to Simon Peter, "Simon, son of Jonah, do you love me more than these?"

He said to him, "Yes, Lord; you know that I have affection for you."

He said to him, "Feed my lambs." He said to him again a second time, "Simon, son of Jonah, do you love me?"

He said to him, "Yes, Lord; you know that I have affection for you."

He said to him, "Tend my sheep." He said to him the third time, "Simon, son of Jonah, do you have affection for me?"

Peter was grieved because he asked him the third time, "Do you have affection for me?" He said to him, "Lord, you know everything. You know that I have affection for you."

Jesus said to him, "Feed my sheep. Most certainly I tell you, when you were young, you dressed yourself, and walked where you wanted to. But when you are old, you will stretch out your hands, and another will dress you, and carry you where you don't want to go."

Now he said this, signifying by what kind of death he would glorify God. When he had said this, he said to him, "Follow me."

Then Peter, turning around, saw a disciple following. This was the disciple whom Jesus loved, the one who had also leaned on Jesus' breast at the supper and asked, "Lord, who is going to betray You?" Peter seeing him, said to Jesus, "Lord, what about this man?"

Jesus said to him, "If I desire that he stay until I come, what is that to you? You follow me." This saying therefore went out among the brothers, that this disciple wouldn't die. Yet Jesus didn't say to him that he wouldn't die, but, "If I desire that he stay until I come, what is that to you?" (John 21:15-23).

Jesus commissions the eleven to make disciples

But the eleven disciples went into Galilee, to the mountain where Jesus had sent them. When they saw him, they bowed down to him, but some doubted. Jesus came to them and spoke to them, saying, "All authority has been given to me in heaven and on earth. Go, and make disciples of all nations, baptizing them in the name of the

Father and of the Son and of the Holy Spirit, teaching them to observe all things that I commanded you. Behold, I am with you always, even to the end of the age" (Matthew 28:16-20).

Jesus returns to heaven

Then he opened their minds, that they might understand the Scriptures. He said to them, "Thus it is written, and thus it was necessary for the Christ to suffer and to rise from the dead the third day, and that repentance and remission of sins should be preached in his name to all the nations, beginning at Jerusalem. You are witnesses of these things. Behold, I send out the promise of my Father on you. But wait in the city of Jerusalem until you are clothed with power from on high."

He led them out as far as Bethany, and he lifted up his hands, and blessed them. While he blessed them, he withdrew from them, and was carried up into heaven. They worshiped him, and returned to Jerusalem with great joy, and were continually in the temple, praising and blessing God (Luke 24:44-53).

There are also many other things which Jesus did, which if they would all be written, I suppose that even the world itself wouldn't have room for the books that would be written (John 21:25).

Note:

Jesus' earthly family tree from Joseph's ancestry

The book of the genealogy of Jesus Christ, the son of David, the son of Abraham. Abraham became the father of Isaac. Isaac became the father of Jacob. Jacob became the father of Judah and his brothers. Judah became the father of Perez and Zerah by Tamar. Perez became the father of Hezron. Hezron became the father of Ram. Ram became the father of Amminadab. Amminadab became the father of Nahshon. Nahshon became the father of Salmon. Salmon became the father of Boaz by Rahab. Boaz became the father of Obed by Ruth. Obed became the father of Jesse. Jesse became the father of King David. David became the father of Solomon by her who had been Uriah's wife. Solomon became the father of Rehoboam. Rehoboam became the father of Abijah. Abijah became the father of Asa. Asa became the father of Jehoshaphat. Jehoshaphat became the father of Joram. Joram became the father of Uzziah. Uzziah became the father of Jotham. Jotham became the father of Ahaz. Ahaz became the father of Hezekiah. Hezekiah became the father of Manasseh. Manasseh became the father of Amon. Amon became the father of Josiah. Josiah became the father of Jechoniah and his brothers, at the time of the exile to Babylon. After the exile to Babylon, Jechoniah became the father of Shealtiel. Shealtiel became the father of Zerubbabel. Zerubbabel became the father of Abiud. Abiud became the father of Eliakim. Eliakim became the father of Azor. Azor became the father of Zadok. Zadok became the father of Achim. Achim became the father of Eliud. Eliud became the father of Eleazar. Eleazar became the father of Matthan. Matthan became the father of Jacob. Jacob became the father of Joseph, the husband of Mary, from whom was born Jesus, who is called Christ. So all the generations from Abraham to David are fourteen generations; from David to the exile to Babylon fourteen generations; and from the carrying away to Babylon to the Christ, fourteen generations (Matthew 1:1-17).

Jesus' earthly family tree from perhaps Mary's ancestry

[Jesus was] the son (as was supposed) of Joseph, the son of Heli, the son of Matthat, the son of Levi, the son of Melchi, the son of Jannai, the son of Joseph, the son of Mattathias, the son of Amos, the son of Nahum, the son of Esli, the son of Naggai, the son of Maath, the son of Mattathias, the son of Semein, the son of Joseph, the son of Judah, the son of Joanan, the son of Rhesa, the son of Zerubbabel, the son of Shealtiel, the son of Neri, the son of Melchi, the son of Addi, the son of Cosam, the son of Elmodam, the son of Er, the son of Jose, the son of Eliezer, the son of Jorim, the son of Matthat, the son of Levi, the son of Simeon, the son of Judah, the son of Joseph, the son of Jonan, the son of Eliakim, the son of Melea, the son of Menan, the son of Mattatha, the son of Nathan, the son of David, the son of Jesse, the son of Obed, the son of Boaz, the son of Salmon, the son of Nahshon, the son of Amminadab, the son of Aram, the son of Hezron, the son of Perez, the son of Judah, the son of Jacob, the son of Isaac, the son of Abraham, the son of Terah, the son of Nahor, the son of Serug, the son of Reu, the son of Peleg, the son of Eber, the son of Shelah, the son of Cainan, the son of Arphaxad, the son of Shem, the son of Noah, the son of Lamech, the son of Methuselah, the son of Enoch, the son of Jared, the son of Mahalaleel, the son of Cainan, the son of Enos, the son of Seth, the son of Adam, the son of God (Luke 3:23-38).

Jesus:
His Lessons

"You have heard that it was said to the ancient ones, 'You shall not murder;' and 'Whoever murders will be in danger of the judgment.' But I tell you, that everyone who is angry with his brother without a cause will be in danger of the judgment; and whoever says to his brother, '*Raca*!' will be in danger of the council; and whoever says, 'You fool!' will be in danger of the fire of Gehenna" (Matthew 5:21-22).

Anxiety

Therefore I tell you, don't be anxious for your life: what you will eat, or what you will drink; nor yet for your body, what you will wear. Isn't life more than food, and the body more than clothing? See the birds of the sky, that they don't sow, neither do they reap, nor gather into barns. Your heavenly Father feeds them. Aren't you of much more value than they?

"Which of you, by being anxious, can add one moment to his lifespan? Why are you anxious about clothing? Consider the lilies of the field, how they grow. They don't toil, neither do they spin, yet I tell you that even Solomon in all his glory was not dressed like one of these. But if God so clothes the grass of the field, which today exists, and tomorrow is thrown into the oven, won't he much more clothe you, you of little faith?

"Therefore don't be anxious, saying, 'What will we eat?', 'What will we drink?' or, 'With what will we be clothed?' For the Gentiles seek after all these things; for your heavenly Father knows that you need all these things. But seek first God's Kingdom, and his righteousness; and all these things will be given to you as well. Therefore don't be anxious for tomorrow, for tomorrow will be anxious for itself. Each day's own evil is sufficient" (Matthew 6:25-34, also Luke 12:22-31).

"Aren't two sparrows sold for [a half hour's wage of a laborer]? Not one of them falls on the ground apart from your Father's will, but the very hairs of your head are all numbered. Therefore don't be afraid. You are of more value than many sparrows" (Matthew 10:29-30, also Luke 12:6-7).

Blessings
> "Blessed are the poor in spirit,
> for theirs is the Kingdom of Heaven.
> Blessed are those who mourn,
> for they shall be comforted.
> Blessed are the gentle,
> for they shall inherit the earth.
> Blessed are those who hunger and thirst after
> righteousness,
> for they shall be filled.
> Blessed are the merciful,
> for they shall obtain mercy.
> Blessed are the pure in heart,
> for they shall see God.
> Blessed are the peacemakers,
> for they shall be called children of God (Matthew 5:3-9).

> "Blessed are you who are poor,
> God's Kingdom is yours.
> Blessed are you who hunger now,
> for you will be filled.
> Blessed are you who weep now,
> for you will laugh.
> Blessed are you when men shall hate you, and when
> they shall exclude and mock you, and throw out your
> name as evil, for the Son of Man's sake.
> Rejoice in that day, and leap for joy, for behold, your

reward is great in heaven, for their fathers did the same thing to the prophets.

"But woe to you who are rich!
For you have received your consolation.
Woe to you, you who are full now,
for you will be hungry.
Woe to you who laugh now,
for you will mourn and weep.
Woe, when men speak well of you,
for their fathers did the same thing to the false prophets" (Luke 6:20-26).

Charity
(See Generosity)

Children

In that hour the disciples came to Jesus, saying, "Who then is greatest in the Kingdom of Heaven?"

Jesus called a little child to himself, and set him in the middle of them, and said, "Most certainly I tell you, unless you turn, and become as little children, you will in no way enter into the Kingdom of Heaven. Whoever therefore humbles himself as this little child, the same is the greatest in the Kingdom of Heaven. Whoever receives one such little child in my name receives me, but whoever causes one of these little ones who believe in me to stumble, it would be better for him that a huge millstone should be hung around his neck, and that he should be sunk in the depths of the sea" (Matthew 18:1-6, Mark 9:33-37, Luke 9:46-48).

"See that you don't despise one of these little ones, for I tell you that in heaven their angels always see the face of my Father who is in heaven. For the Son of Man came to save that which was lost.

"What do you think? If a man has one hundred sheep, and one of them goes astray, doesn't he leave the ninety-nine, go to the mountains, and seek that which has gone astray? If he finds it, most certainly I tell you, he rejoices over it more than over the ninety-nine which have not gone astray. Even so it is not the will of your Father who is in heaven that one of these little ones should perish (Matthew 18:10-14, also Luke 15:3-6).

They were also bringing their babies to him, that he might touch them. But when the disciples saw it, they rebuked them. Jesus summoned them, saying, "Allow the little children to come to me, and don't hinder them, for God's Kingdom belongs to such as these. Most certainly, I tell you, whoever doesn't receive God's Kingdom like a little child, he will in no way enter into it" (Luke 18:15-17, also Matthew 19:13-15, Mark 10:13-16).

Confession of Jesus
"Everyone therefore who confesses me before men, him I will also confess before my Father who is in heaven. But whoever denies me before men, him I will also deny before my Father who is in heaven" (Matthew 10:32-33, also Luke 12:8-9).

Correction
"If your brother sins against you, go, show him his fault between you and him alone. If he listens to you, you have gained back your brother. But if he doesn't listen, take one or two more with you, that at the mouth of two or three witnesses every word may be established. If he refuses to listen to them, tell it to the assembly. If he refuses to hear the assembly also, let him be to you as a Gentile or a tax collector" (Matthew 18:15-17, also Luke 17:3).

Disasters
"Now there were some present at the same time who told him about the Galileans, whose blood Pilate had mixed with their sacrifices. Jesus answered them, "Do you think that these Galileans were worse sinners than all the other Galileans, because they suffered such things? I tell you, no, but unless you repent, you will all perish in the same way. Or those eighteen, on whom the tower in Siloam fell, and killed them; do you think that they were worse offenders than all the men who dwell in Jerusalem? I tell you, no, but, unless you repent, you will all perish in the same way" (Luke 13:1-5).

"All authority has been given to me in heaven and on earth. Go, and make disciples of all nations, baptizing them in the name of the Father and of the Son and of the Holy Spirit, teaching them to observe all things that I commanded you. Behold, I am with you always, even to the end of the age" (Matthew 28:18-20, also Mark 15:14-15, John 19:21-22).

"If anyone desires to come after me, let him deny himself, take up his cross, and follow me. For whoever desires to save his life will lose it, but whoever will lose his life for my sake, the same will save it. For what does it profit a man if he gains the whole world, and loses or forfeits his own self? For whoever will be ashamed of me and of my words, of him will the Son of Man be ashamed, when he comes in his glory, and the glory of the Father, and of the holy angels" (Luke 9:23-26, also Matthew 16:24-26, Mark 8:34-38).

As they went on the way, a certain man said to him, "I want to follow you wherever you go, Lord."

Jesus said to him, "The foxes have holes, and the birds of the sky have nests, but the Son of Man has no place to lay his head."

He said to another, "Follow me!"

But he said, "Lord, allow me first to go and bury my father."

But Jesus said to him, "Leave the dead to bury their own dead, but you go and announce God's Kingdom."

Another also said, "I want to follow you, Lord, but first allow me to say good-bye to those who are at my house."

But Jesus said to him, "No one, having put his hand to the plow, and looking back, is fit for God's Kingdom" (Luke 9:57-62, also Matthew 8:19-22).

"If anyone comes to me, and doesn't disregard his own father, mother, wife, children, brothers, and sisters, yes, and his own life also, he can't be my disciple. Whoever doesn't bear his own cross, and come after me, can't be my disciple. For which of you, desiring to build a tower, doesn't first sit down and count the cost, to see if he has enough to complete it? Or perhaps, when he has laid a foundation, and is not able to finish, everyone who sees begins to mock him, saying, 'This man began to build, and wasn't able to finish.' Or what king, as he goes to encounter another king in war, will not sit down first and consider whether he is able with ten thousand to meet him who comes against him with twenty thousand? Or else, while the other is yet a great way off, he sends an envoy, and asks for conditions of peace. So therefore whoever of you who doesn't renounce all that he has, he can't be my disciple" (Luke 14:26-33, also Matthew 10:37-39).

Divorce

"It was also said, 'Whoever shall put away his wife, let him give her a writing of divorce,' but I tell you that whoever puts away his wife, except for the cause of sexual immorality, makes her an adulteress; and whoever marries her when she is put away commits adultery (Matthew 5:31-32, also 19:3-9; Mark 10:2-12; Luke 16:18).

(See also Marriage)

End of the Age

Jesus went out from the temple, and was going on his way. His disciples came to him to show him the buildings of the temple. But he answered them, "You see all of these things, don't you? Most certainly I tell you, there will not be left here one stone on another, that will not be thrown down."

As he sat on the Mount of Olives, the disciples came to him privately, saying, "Tell us, when will these things be? What is the sign of your coming, and of the end of the age?"

Jesus answered them, "Be careful that no one leads you astray. For many will come in my name, saying, 'I am the Christ,' and will lead many astray. You will hear of wars and rumors of wars. See that you aren't troubled, for all this must happen, but the end is not yet. For nation will rise against nation, and kingdom against kingdom; and there will be famines, plagues, and earthquakes in various places. But all these things are the beginning of birth pains. Then they will deliver you up to oppression, and will kill you. You will be hated by all of the nations for my name's sake. Then many will stumble, and will deliver up one another, and will hate one another. Many false prophets will arise, and will lead many astray. Because iniquity will be multiplied, the love of many will grow cold. But he who endures to the end, the same will be saved. This Good News of the Kingdom will be preached in the whole world for a testimony to all the nations, and then the end will come.

"When, therefore, you see the abomination of desolation, which was spoken of through Daniel the prophet, standing in the holy place (let the reader understand), then let those who are in Judea flee to the mountains. Let him who is on the housetop not go down to take out things that are in his house. Let him who is in the field not return back to get his clothes. But woe to those who are with child and to nursing mothers in those days! Pray that your flight will not be in the winter, nor on a Sabbath, for then there will be great oppression, such as has not been from the beginning of the world until now, no, nor ever will be. Unless those days had been shortened, no flesh would have been saved. But for the sake of the chosen ones, those days will be shortened.

"Then if any man tells you, 'Behold, here is the Christ,' or, 'There,' don't believe it. For there will arise false christs, and false prophets, and they will show great signs and wonders, so as to lead astray, if possible, even the chosen ones.

"Behold, I have told you beforehand. If therefore they tell you, 'Behold, he is in the wilderness,' don't go out; 'Behold, he is in the inner rooms,' don't believe it. For as the lightning flashes from the east, and is seen even to the west, so will be the coming of the Son of Man. For wherever the carcass is, there is where the vultures gather together. But immediately after the oppression of those days, the sun will be darkened, the moon will not give its light, the stars will fall from the sky, and the powers of the heavens will be shaken; and then the sign of the Son of Man will appear in the sky. Then all the tribes of the earth will mourn, and they will see the Son of Man coming on the clouds of the sky with power and great glory. He will send out his angels with a great sound of a trumpet, and they will gather together his chosen ones from the four winds, from one end of the sky to the other.

"Now from the fig tree learn this parable. When its branch has now become tender, and produces its leaves, you know that the summer is near. Even so you also, when you see all these things, know that it is near, even at the doors. Most certainly I tell you, this generation will not pass away, until all these things are accomplished. Heaven and earth will pass away, but my words will not pass away. But no one knows of that day and hour, not even the angels of heaven, but my Father only.

"As the days of Noah were, so will be the coming of the Son of Man. For as in those days which were before the flood they were eating and drinking, marrying and giving in marriage, until the day that Noah entered into the ship, and they didn't know until the flood came, and took them all away, so will be the coming of the Son of Man. Then two men will be in the field: one will be taken and one will be left; two women grinding at the mill, one will be taken and one will be left. Watch therefore, for you don't know in what hour your Lord comes. But know this, that if the master of the house had known in what watch of the night the thief was coming, he would have watched, and would not have allowed his house to be broken into. Therefore also be ready, for in an hour that you don't expect, the Son of Man will come.

"Who then is the faithful and wise servant, whom his lord has set over his household, to give them their food in due season? Blessed is that servant whom his lord finds doing so when he comes. Most certainly I tell you that he will set him over all that he has. But if that evil servant should say in his heart, 'My lord is delaying his coming,' and begins to beat his fellow servants, and eat and drink with the drunkards, the lord of that servant will come in a day when he doesn't expect it, and in an hour when he doesn't know it, and will cut him in pieces, and appoint his portion with the hypocrites. There is where the weeping and grinding of teeth will be" (Matthew 24:1-51; also Mark 13:3-37; Luke 17:22-37, 21:7-36).

Eternal life

"Enter in by the narrow gate; for wide is the gate and broad is the way that leads to destruction, and many are those who enter in by it.

How narrow is the gate, and restricted is the way that leads to life! Few are those who find it" (Matthew 7:13-14, also Luke 13:24).

On that day Sadducees (those who say that there is no resurrection) came to him. They asked him, saying, "Teacher, Moses said, 'If a man dies, having no children, his brother shall marry his wife, and raise up offspring for his brother.' Now there were with us seven brothers. The first married and died, and having no offspring left his wife to his brother. In the same way, the second also, and the third, to the seventh. After them all, the woman died. In the resurrection therefore, whose wife will she be of the seven? For they all had her."

But Jesus answered them, "You are mistaken, not knowing the Scriptures, nor the power of God. For in the resurrection they neither marry, nor are given in marriage, but are like God's angels in heaven. But concerning the resurrection of the dead, haven't you read that which was spoken to you by God, saying, 'I am the God of Abraham, and the God of Isaac, and the God of Jacob?' God is not the God of the dead, but of the living" (Matthew 22:23-32).

Behold, a certain lawyer stood up and tested him, saying, "Teacher, what shall I do to inherit eternal life?"

He said to him, "What is written in the law? How do you read it?"

He answered, "You shall love the Lord your God with all your heart, with all your soul, with all your strength, and with all your mind; and your neighbor as yourself."

He said to him, "You have answered correctly. Do this, and you will live."

But he, desiring to justify himself, asked Jesus, "Who is my neighbor?" (Luke 10:25-29)

[Jesus answers with **Parable of Good Samaritan** (Luke 10:30-37).]

"Most certainly I tell you, he who hears my word, and believes him who sent me, has eternal life, and doesn't come into judgment, but has passed out of death into life. Most certainly, I tell you, the hour comes, and now is, when the dead will hear the Son of God's voice; and those who hear will live. For as the Father has life in himself, even so he gave to the Son also to have life in himself" (John 5:24-26).

"It is the spirit who gives life. The flesh profits nothing. The words that I speak to you are spirit, and are life. But there are some of you who don't believe." For Jesus knew from the beginning who they were who didn't believe, and who it was who would betray him. He said, "For this cause have I said to you that no one can come to me, unless it is given to him by my Father.

At this, many of his disciples went back, and walked no more with him. Jesus said therefore to the twelve, "You don't also want to go away, do you?"

Simon Peter answered him, "Lord, to whom would we go? You have the words of eternal life. We have come to believe and know that you are the Christ, the Son of the living God" (John 6:63-65).

Jesus answered them, "Most certainly I tell you, everyone who commits sin is the bondservant of sin. A bondservant doesn't live in the house forever. A son remains forever. If therefore the Son makes you free, you will be free indeed" (John 8:34-36).

"Don't let your heart be troubled. Believe in God. Believe also in me. In my Father's house are many homes. If it weren't so, I would have told you. I am going to prepare a place for you. If I go and prepare a place for you, I will come again, and will receive you to myself; that where I am, you may be there also. Where I go, you know, and you know the way" (John 14:1-4).

Faith

"For most certainly I tell you, if you have faith as a grain of mustard seed, you will tell this mountain, 'Move from here to there,' and it will move; and nothing will be impossible for you" (Matthew 17:20b).

"All things, whatever you ask in prayer, believing, you will receive" (Matthew 21:22).

False Prophets

"Beware of false prophets, who come to you in sheep's clothing, but inwardly are ravening wolves. By their fruits you will know them. Do you gather grapes from thorns, or figs from thistles? Even so, every good tree produces good fruit; but the corrupt tree produces evil fruit. A good tree can't produce evil fruit, neither can a corrupt tree produce good fruit. Every tree that doesn't grow good fruit is cut down, and thrown into the fire. Therefore by their fruits you will know them. Not everyone who says to me, 'Lord, Lord,' will enter into the Kingdom of Heaven; but he who does the will of my Father who is in heaven. Many will tell me in that day, 'Lord, Lord, didn't we prophesy in your name, in your name cast out demons, and in your name do many mighty works?' Then I will tell them, 'I never knew you. Depart from me, you who work iniquity'" (Matthew 7:15-23; also Luke 6:43-45, 13:26-27).

Fasting

"Moreover when you fast, don't be like the hypocrites, with sad faces. For they disfigure their faces, that they may be seen by men to be fasting. Most certainly I tell you, they have received their reward. But you, when you fast, anoint your head, and wash your face; so that you are not seen by men to be fasting, but by your Father who is in secret, and your Father, who sees in secret, will reward you" (Matthew 6:16-18).

Fear
(See Anxiety)

Forgiveness

"You have heard that it was said, 'An eye for an eye, and a tooth for a tooth.' But I tell you, don't resist him who is evil; but whoever strikes you on your right cheek, turn to him the other also. If anyone sues you to take away your coat, let him have your cloak also. Whoever compels you to go one mile, go with him two. Give to him who asks you, and don't turn away him who desires to borrow from you (Matthew 5:38-42).

"For if you forgive men their trespasses, your heavenly Father will also forgive you. But if you don't forgive men their trespasses, neither will your Father forgive your trespasses (Matthew 6:14-15).

Then Peter came and said to him, "Lord, how often shall my brother sin against me, and I forgive him? Until seven times?"

Jesus said to him, "I don't tell you until seven times, but, until seventy times seven (Matthew 18:21-22).

[See **Parable of the Unforgiving Servant** (Matthew 18:23-35).]

Freedom

Jesus therefore said to those Jews who had believed him, "If you remain in my word, then you are truly my disciples. You will know the truth, and the truth will make you free."

They answered him, "We are Abraham's offspring, and have never been in bondage to anyone. How do you say, 'You will be made free'?"

Jesus answered them, "Most certainly I tell you, everyone who commits sin is the bondservant of sin. A bondservant doesn't live in the house forever. A son remains forever. If therefore the Son makes you free, you will be free indeed" (John 8:31-36).

Friendship with Jesus

His mother and his brothers came, and standing outside, they sent to him, calling him. A multitude was sitting around him, and they told him, "Behold, your mother, your brothers, and your sisters are outside looking for you."

He answered them, "Who are my mother and my brothers?" Looking around at those who sat around him, he said, "Behold, my mother and my brothers! For whoever does the will of God, the same is my brother, and my sister, and mother" (Mark 3:31-35, also Matthew 12:46-50, Luke 8:19-21).

"You are my friends, if you do whatever I command you. No longer do I call you servants, for the servant doesn't know what his lord does. But I have called you friends, for everything that I heard from my Father, I have made known to you" (John 15:14-15).

Fruit

"I am the true vine, and my Father is the farmer. Every branch in me that doesn't bear fruit, he takes away. Every branch that bears fruit, he prunes, that it may bear more fruit. You are already pruned clean because of the word which I have spoken to you. Remain in me, and I in you. As the branch can't bear fruit by itself, unless it remains in the vine, so neither can you, unless you remain in me. I am the vine. You are the branches. He who remains in me, and I in him, the same bears much fruit, for apart from me you can do nothing. If a man doesn't remain in me, he is thrown out as a branch, and is withered; and they gather them, throw them into the fire, and they are burned. If you remain in me, and my words remain in you, you will ask whatever you desire, and it will be done for you.

"In this is my Father glorified, that you bear much fruit; and so you will be my disciples" (John 15:1-8).

Generosity

"Be careful that you don't do your charitable giving before men, to be seen by them, or else you have no reward from your Father who is in heaven. Therefore when you do merciful deeds, don't sound a trumpet before yourself, as the hypocrites do in the synagogues and in the streets, that they may get glory from men. Most certainly I tell you, they have received their reward. But when you do merciful deeds, don't let your left hand know what your right hand does, so that your merciful deeds may be in secret, then your Father who sees in secret will reward you openly" (Matthew 6:1-4).

"He who receives you receives me, and he who receives me receives him who sent me. He who receives a prophet in the name of a prophet will receive a prophet's reward. He who receives a righteous man in the name of a righteous man will receive a righteous man's reward. Whoever gives one of these little ones just a cup of cold water to drink in the name of a disciple, most certainly I tell you he will in no way lose his reward" (Matthew 10:40-42, also Mark 9:41).

"Give, and it will be given to you: good measure, pressed down, shaken together, and running over, will be given to you. For with the same measure you measure it will be measured back to you" (Luke 6:38).

He spoke a parable to those who were invited, when he noticed how they chose the best seats, and said to them, He also said to the one who had invited him, "When you make a dinner or a supper, don't call your friends, nor your brothers, nor your kinsmen, nor rich neighbors, or perhaps they might also return the favor, and pay you back. But when you make a feast, ask the poor, the maimed, the lame, or the blind; and you will be blessed, because they don't have the resources to repay you. For you will be repaid in the resurrection of the righteous" (Luke 14:7-14).

[See **Parable of Sheep and Goats** (Matthew 25: 31-46).]

Heaven
(See Eternal life)

Holy Spirit
"If you then, being evil, know how to give good gifts to your children, how much more will your heavenly Father give the Holy Spirit to those who ask him?" (Luke 11:13).

"If anyone is thirsty, let him come to me and drink! He who believes in me, as the Scripture has said, from within him will flow rivers of living water." But he said this about the Spirit, which those believing in him were to receive. For the Holy Spirit was not yet given, because Jesus wasn't yet glorified" (John 7:37-39).
"I will pray to the Father, and he will give you another Counselor, that he may be with you forever,—the Spirit of truth, whom the world can't receive; for it doesn't see him, neither knows

him. You know him, for he lives with you, and will be in you. I will not leave you orphans. I will come to you. Yet a little while, and the world will see me no more; but you will see me. Because I live, you will live also. In that day you will know that I am in my Father, and you in me, and I in you" (John 14:16-20).

"I have said these things to you, while still living with you. But the Counselor, the Holy Spirit, whom the Father will send in my name, he will teach you all things, and will remind you of all that I said to you.

"When the Counselor has come, whom I will send to you from the Father, the Spirit of truth, who proceeds from the Father, he will testify about me. You will also testify, because you have been with me from the beginning" (John 14:25-26).

"But I have told you these things, so that when the time comes, you may remember that I told you about them. I didn't tell you these things from the beginning, because I was with you. But now I am going to him who sent me, and none of you asks me, 'Where are you going?' But because I have told you these things, sorrow has filled your heart. Nevertheless I tell you the truth: It is to your advantage that I go away, for if I don't go away, the Counselor won't come to you. But if I go, I will send him to you. When he has come, he will convict the world about sin, about righteousness, and about judgment; about sin, because they don't believe in me; about righteousness, because I am going to my Father, and you won't see me any more; about judgment, because the prince of this world has been judged (John 16:4-11).

Humility

"When you are invited by anyone to a marriage feast, don't sit in the best seat, since perhaps someone more honorable than you might be invited by him, and he who invited both of you would come and tell you, 'Make room for this person.' Then you would begin, with shame, to take the lowest place. But when you are invited, go and sit in the lowest place, so that when he who invited you comes, he may tell you, 'Friend, move up higher.' Then you will be honored in the presence of all who sit at the table with you. For everyone who exalts himself will be humbled, and whoever humbles himself will be exalted" (Luke 14:8-11).

"Two men went up into the temple to pray; one was a Pharisee, and the other was a tax collector. The Pharisee stood and prayed to himself like this: 'God, I thank you, that I am not like the rest of men, extortionists, unrighteous, adulterers, or even like this tax collector. I fast twice a week. I give tithes of all that I get.' But the tax collector, standing far away, wouldn't even lift up his eyes to heaven, but beat his breast, saying, 'God, be merciful to me, a sinner!' I tell you, this man went down to his house justified rather than the other; for everyone who exalts himself will be humbled, but he who humbles himself will be exalted" (Luke 18:10-14).

Hypocrisy

Then Pharisees and scribes came to Jesus from Jerusalem, saying, "Why do your disciples disobey the tradition of the elders? For they don't wash their hands when they eat bread."

He answered them, "Why do you also disobey the commandment of God because of your tradition? For God commanded, 'Honor your father and your mother,' and, 'He who speaks evil of father or mother, let him be put to death.' But you say, 'Whoever may tell his father or his mother, "Whatever help you might otherwise have gotten from me is a gift devoted to God," he shall not honor his father or mother.' You have made the commandment of God void because of your tradition. You hypocrites! Well did Isaiah prophesy of you, saying,

> 'These people draw near to me with their mouth,
> and honor me with their lips;
> but their heart is far from me.
> And in vain do they worship me,
> teaching as doctrine rules made by men.'"

He summoned the multitude, and said to them, "Hear, and understand. That which enters into the mouth doesn't defile the man; but that which proceeds out of the mouth, this defiles the man."

Then the disciples came, and said to him, "Do you know that the Pharisees were offended, when they heard this saying?"

But he answered, "Every plant which my heavenly Father didn't plant will be uprooted. Leave them alone. They are blind guides of the blind. If the blind guide the blind, both will fall into a pit."

Peter answered him, "Explain the parable to us."

So Jesus said, "Do you also still not understand? Don't you understand that whatever goes into the mouth passes into the belly, and then out of the body? But the things which proceed out of the mouth come out of the heart, and they defile the man. For out of the heart come evil thoughts, murders, adulteries, sexual sins, thefts, false testimony, and blasphemies. These are the things which defile the man; but to eat with unwashed hands doesn't defile the man" (Matthew 15:1-20, also Mark 7:1-23).

Then Jesus spoke to the multitudes and to his disciples, saying, "The scribes and the Pharisees sat on Moses' seat. All things therefore whatever they tell you to observe, observe and do, but don't do their works; for they say, and don't do. For they bind heavy burdens that are grievous to be borne, and lay them on men's shoulders; but they themselves will not lift a finger to help them. But all their works they do to be seen by men. They make their phylacteries broad, enlarge the fringes of their garments, and love the place of honor at feasts, the best seats in the synagogues, the salutations in the marketplaces, and to be called 'Rabbi, Rabbi' by men. But don't you be called 'Rabbi,' for one is your teacher, the Christ, and all of you are brothers. Call no man on the earth your father, for one is your Father, he who is in heaven. Neither be called masters, for one is your master, the Christ. But he who is greatest among you will be your servant. Whoever exalts himself will be humbled, and whoever humbles himself will be exalted.

"Woe to you, scribes and Pharisees, hypocrites! For you devour widows' houses, and as a pretense you make long prayers. Therefore you will receive greater condemnation.

"But woe to you, scribes and Pharisees, hypocrites! Because you shut up the Kingdom of Heaven against men; for you don't enter in yourselves, neither do you allow those who are entering in to enter. Woe to you, scribes and Pharisees, hypocrites! For you travel around by sea and land to make one proselyte; and when he becomes one, you make him twice as much of a son of Gehenna as yourselves.

"Woe to you, you blind guides, who say, 'Whoever swears by the temple, it is nothing; but whoever swears by the gold of the temple, he is obligated.' You blind fools! For which is greater, the gold, or the temple that sanctifies the gold? 'Whoever swears by the altar, it is nothing; but whoever swears by the gift that is on it, he is obligated?' You blind fools! For which is greater, the gift, or the altar that sanctifies the gift? He therefore who swears by the altar, swears by it, and by everything on it. He who swears by the temple, swears by it, and by him who was living in it. He who swears by heaven, swears by the throne of God, and by him who sits on it.

"Woe to you, scribes and Pharisees, hypocrites! For you tithe mint, dill, and cumin, and have left undone the weightier matters of the law: justice, mercy, and faith. But you ought to have done these, and not to have left the other undone. You blind guides, who strain out a gnat, and swallow a camel!

"Woe to you, scribes and Pharisees, hypocrites! For you clean the outside of the cup and of the platter, but within they are full of extortion and unrighteousness. You blind Pharisee, first clean the inside of the cup and of the platter, that its outside may become clean also.

"Woe to you, scribes and Pharisees, hypocrites! For you are like whitened tombs, which outwardly appear beautiful, but inwardly are full of dead men's bones, and of all uncleanness. Even so you also outwardly appear righteous to men, but inwardly you are full of hypocrisy and iniquity.

"Woe to you, scribes and Pharisees, hypocrites! For you build the tombs of the prophets, and decorate the tombs of the righteous, and say, 'If we had lived in the days of our fathers, we wouldn't have been partakers with them in the blood of the prophets.' Therefore you testify to yourselves that you are children of those who killed the prophets. Fill up, then, the measure of your fathers. You serpents, you offspring of vipers, how will you escape the judgment of Gehenna? Therefore behold, I send to you prophets, wise men, and scribes. Some of them you will kill and crucify; and some of them you will scourge in your synagogues, and persecute from city to city; that on you may come all the righteous blood shed on the earth, from the blood of righteous Abel to the blood of Zachariah son of Barachiah, whom you killed between the sanctuary and the altar. Most certainly I tell you, all these things will come upon this generation" (Matthew 23:1-36; also Mark 12:38-40; Luke 11:37-52).

"Beware of the yeast of the Pharisees, which is hypocrisy. But there is nothing covered up, that will not be revealed, nor hidden, that will not be known. Therefore whatever you have said in the darkness will be heard in the light. What you have spoken in the ear in the inner rooms will be proclaimed on the housetops" (Luke 12:1-3).

"Beware of the scribes, who like to walk in long robes, and love greetings in the marketplaces, the best seats in the synagogues, and the best places at feasts; who devour widows' houses, and for a pretense make long prayers: these will receive greater condemnation" (Luke 20:46-47).

Jesus teaches about himself

Now when Jesus came into the parts of Caesarea Philippi, he asked his disciples, saying, "Who do men say that I, the Son of Man, am?"

They said, "Some say John the Baptizer, some, Elijah, and others, Jeremiah, or one of the prophets."

He said to them, "But who do you say that I am?"

Simon Peter answered, "You are the Christ, the Son of the living God."

Jesus answered him, "Blessed are you, Simon Bar Jonah, for flesh and blood has not revealed this to you, but my Father who is in heaven. I also tell you that you are Peter, and on this rock I will build my assembly, and the gates of Hades will not prevail against it. I will give to you the keys of the Kingdom of Heaven, and whatever you bind on earth will have been bound in heaven; and whatever you release on earth will have been released in heaven." Then he commanded the disciples that they should tell no one that he was Jesus the Christ (Matthew 16:13-20, also Mark 8:27-30, Luke 9:18-21).

Now when John heard in the prison the works of Christ, he sent two of his disciples and said to him, "Are you he who comes, or should we look for another?"

Jesus answered them, "Go and tell John the things which you hear and see: the blind receive their sight, the lame walk, the lepers are cleansed, the deaf hear, the dead are raised up, and the poor have good news preached to them. Blessed is he who finds no occasion for stumbling in me" (Matthew 11:2-6, also Luke 7:18-35).

At that time, Jesus answered, "I thank you, Father, Lord of heaven and earth, that you hid these things from the wise and understanding, and revealed them to infants. Yes, Father, for so it was well-pleasing in your sight. All things have been delivered to me by my Father. No one knows the Son, except the Father; neither does anyone know the Father, except the Son, and he to whom the Son desires to reveal him" (Matthew 11:25-27, also Luke 10:22).

At that time, Jesus went on the Sabbath day through the grain fields. His disciples were hungry and began to pluck heads of grain and to eat. But the Pharisees, when they saw it, said to him, "Behold, your disciples do what is not lawful to do on the Sabbath."

But he said to them, "Haven't you read what David did, when he was hungry, and those who were with him; how he entered into God's house, and ate the show bread, which was not lawful for him to eat, neither for those who were with him, but only for the priests? Or have you not read in the law, that on the Sabbath day, the priests in the temple profane the Sabbath, and are guiltless? But I tell you that one greater than the temple is here. But if you had known what this means, 'I desire mercy, and not sacrifice,' you would not have condemned the guiltless. For the Son of Man is Lord of the Sabbath" (Matthew 12:1-8, also Mark 2:23-28, Luke 6:1-5).

"Where two or three are gathered together in my name, there I am in the middle of them" (Matthew 18:20).

The scribes who came down from Jerusalem said, "[Jesus] has Beelzebul," and, "By the prince of the demons he casts out the demons."

[Jesus] summoned them, and said to them in parables, "How can Satan cast out Satan? If a kingdom is divided against itself, that kingdom cannot stand. If a house is divided against itself, that house cannot stand. If Satan has risen up against himself, and is divided, he can't stand, but has an end. But no one can enter into the house of the strong man to plunder, unless he first binds the strong man; and then he will plunder his house. Most certainly I tell you, all sins of the descendants of man will be forgiven, including their blasphemies with which they may blaspheme; but whoever may blaspheme against the Holy Spirit never has forgiveness, but is subject to eternal condemnation"—because they said, "He has an unclean spirit" (Mark 3:22-30; also Luke 11:14-23, 12:10).

"This is an evil generation. It seeks after a sign. No sign will be given to it but the sign of Jonah, the prophet. For even as Jonah became a sign to the Ninevites, so will also the Son of Man be to this generation. The Queen of the South will rise up in the judgment with the men of this generation, and will condemn them: for she came from the ends of the earth to hear the wisdom of Solomon; and behold, one greater than Solomon is here. The men of Nineveh will stand up in the judgment with this generation, and will condemn it: for they repented at the preaching of Jonah, and behold, one greater than Jonah is here" (Luke 11:29-32, also Matthew 12:38-42, Mark 8:12).

The [Samaritan] woman said to him, "I know that Messiah comes, he who is called Christ. When he has come, he will declare to us all things."

Jesus said to her, "I am he, the one who speaks to you" (John 4:25-26).

But Jesus answered [the Jews in the Temple], "My Father is still working, so I am working, too." For this cause therefore the Jews sought all the more to kill him, because he not only broke the Sabbath, but also called God his own Father, making himself equal with God. Jesus therefore answered them, "Most certainly, I tell you, the Son can do nothing of himself, but what he sees the Father doing. For whatever things he does, these the Son also does likewise. For the Father has affection for the Son, and shows him all things that he himself does. He will show him greater works than these, that you may marvel. For as the Father raises the dead and gives them life, even so the Son also gives life to whom he desires. For the Father judges no one, but he has given all judgment to the Son, that all may honor the Son, even as they honor the Father. He who doesn't honor the Son doesn't honor the Father who sent him.

"Most certainly I tell you, he who hears my word, and believes him who sent me, has eternal life, and doesn't come into judgment, but has passed out of death into life. Most certainly, I tell you, the hour comes, and now is, when the dead will hear the Son of God's voice; and those who hear will live. For as the Father has life in himself, even so he gave to the Son also to have life in himself. He also gave him authority to execute judgment, because he is a son of man. Don't marvel at this, for the hour comes, in which all that are in the tombs will hear his voice, and will come out; those who have done good, to the resurrection of life; and those who have done evil, to the resurrection of judgment. I can of myself do nothing. As I hear, I judge, and my judgment is righteous; because I don't seek my own will, but the will of my Father who sent me.

"If I testify about myself, my witness is not valid. It is another who testifies about me. I know that the testimony which he testifies about me is true. You have sent to John, and he has testified to the truth. But the testimony which I receive is not from man. However, I say these things that you may be saved. He was the burning and shining lamp, and you were willing to rejoice for a while in his light. But the testimony which I have is greater than that of John, for the works which the Father gave me to accomplish, the very works that I do, testify about me, that the Father has sent me. The Father himself, who sent me, has testified about me. You have neither heard his voice at any time, nor seen his form. You don't have his word living in you; because you don't believe him whom he sent.

"You search the Scriptures, because you think that in them you have eternal life; and these are they which testify about me. Yet you will not come to me, that you may have life. I don't receive glory from men. But I know you, that you don't have God's love in yourselves. I have come in my Father's name, and you don't receive me. If another comes in his own name, you will receive him. How can you believe, who receive glory from one another, and you don't seek the glory that comes from the only God?

"Don't think that I will accuse you to the Father. There is one who accuses you, even Moses, on whom you have set your hope. For if you believed Moses, you would believe me; for he wrote about me. But if you don't believe his writings, how will you believe my words?" (John 5:17-47).

Jesus answered [the multitude he had miraculously fed], "Most certainly I tell you, you seek me, not because you saw signs, but because you ate of the loaves, and were filled. Don't work for the food which perishes, but for the food which remains to eternal life, which the Son of Man will give to you. For God the Father has sealed him."

They said therefore to him, "What must we do, that we may work the works of God?"

Jesus answered them, "This is the work of God, that you believe in him whom he has sent."

They said therefore to him, "What then do you do for a sign, that we may see, and believe you? What work do you do? Our fathers ate the manna in the wilderness. As it is written, 'He gave them bread out of heaven to eat.'"

Jesus therefore said to them, "Most certainly, I tell you, it wasn't Moses who gave you the bread out of heaven, but my Father gives you the true bread out of heaven. For the bread of God is that which comes down out of heaven, and gives life to the world."

They said therefore to him, "Lord, always give us this bread."

Jesus said to them, "I am the bread of life. He who comes to me will not be hungry, and he who believes in me will never be thirsty. But I told you that you have seen me, and yet you don't believe. All those whom the Father gives me will come to me. He who comes to me I will in no way throw out. For I have come down from heaven, not to do my own will, but the will of him who sent me. This is the will of my Father who sent me, that of all he has given to me I should lose nothing, but should raise him up at the last day. This is the will of the one who sent me, that everyone who sees the Son, and believes in him, should have eternal life; and I will raise him up at the last day."

The Jews therefore murmured concerning him, because he said, "I am the bread which came down out of heaven." They said, "Isn't this Jesus, the son of Joseph, whose father and mother we know? How then does he say, 'I have come down out of heaven?'"

Therefore Jesus answered them, "Don't murmur among yourselves. No one can come to me unless the Father who sent me draws him, and I will raise him up in the last day. It is written in the prophets, 'They will all be taught by God.' Therefore everyone who hears from the Father, and has learned, comes to me. Not that anyone has seen the Father, except he who is from God. He has seen the Father. Most certainly, I tell you, he who believes in me has eternal life. I am the bread of life. Your fathers ate the manna in the wilderness, and they died. This is the bread which comes down out of heaven, that anyone may eat of it and not die. I am the living bread which came down out of heaven. If anyone eats of this bread, he will live forever. Yes, the bread which I will give for the life of the world is my flesh."

The Jews therefore contended with one another, saying, "How can this man give us his flesh to eat?"

Jesus therefore said to them, "Most certainly I tell you, unless you eat the flesh of the Son of Man and drink his blood, you don't have life in yourselves. He who eats my flesh and drinks my blood has eternal life, and I will raise him up at the last day. For my flesh is food indeed, and my blood is drink indeed. He who eats my flesh and drinks my blood lives in me, and I in him. As the living Father sent me, and I live because of the Father; so he who feeds on me, he will also live because of me. This is the bread which came down out of heaven—not as our fathers ate the manna, and died. He who eats this bread will live forever" (John 6:26-58).

"My teaching is not mine, but his who sent me. If anyone desires to do his will, he will know about the teaching, whether it is from God, or if I am speaking from myself. He who speaks from himself seeks his own glory, but he who seeks the glory of him who sent him is true, and no unrighteousness is in him" (John 7:16-18).

"I am the light of the world. He who follows me will not walk in the darkness, but will have the light of life."

The Pharisees therefore said to him, "You testify about yourself. Your testimony is not valid."

Jesus answered them, "Even if I testify about myself, my testimony is true, for I know where I came from, and where I am going; but you don't know where I came from, or where I am going. You judge according to the flesh. I judge no one. Even if I do judge, my judgment is true, for I am not alone, but I am with the Father who sent me. It's also written in your law that the testimony of two people is valid. I am one who testifies about myself, and the Father who sent me testifies about me."

They said therefore to him, "Where is your Father?"

Jesus answered, "You know neither me, nor my Father. If you knew me, you would know my Father also." Jesus spoke these words in the treasury, as he taught in the temple. Yet no one arrested him, because his hour had not yet come. Jesus said therefore again to them, "I am going away, and you will seek me, and you will die in your sins. Where I go, you can't come."

The Jews therefore said, "Will he kill himself, that he says, 'Where I am going, you can't come'?"

He said to them, "You are from beneath. I am from above. You are of this world. I am not of this world. I said therefore to you that you will die in your sins; for unless you believe that I am he, you will die in your sins."

They said therefore to him, "Who are you?"

Jesus said to them, "Just what I have been saying to you from the beginning. I have many things to speak and to judge concerning you. However he who sent me is true; and the things which I heard from him, these I say to the world" (John 8:12-26).

Therefore Jesus said to [the scribes and the Pharisees], "If God were your father, you would love me, for I came out and have come from God. For I haven't come of myself, but he sent me. Why don't you understand my speech? Because you can't hear my word. You are of your father, the devil, and you want to do the desires of your father. He was a murderer from the beginning, and doesn't stand in the truth, because there is no truth in him. When he speaks a lie, he speaks on his own; for he is a liar, and its father. But because I tell the truth, you don't believe me. Which of you convicts me of sin? If I tell the truth, why do you not believe me? He who is of God hears the words of God. For this cause you don't hear, because you are not of God."

Then the Jews answered him, "Don't we say well that you are a Samaritan, and have a demon?"

Jesus answered, "I don't have a demon, but I honor my Father, and you dishonor me. But I don't seek my own glory. There is one who seeks and judges. Most certainly, I tell you, if a person keeps my word, he will never see death."

Then the Jews said to him, "Now we know that you have a demon. Abraham died, and the prophets; and you say, 'If a man keeps my word, he will never taste of death.' Are you greater than our father, Abraham, who died? The prophets died. Who do you make yourself out to be?"

Jesus answered, "If I glorify myself, my glory is nothing. It is my Father who glorifies me, of whom you say that he is our God. You have not known him, but I know him. If I said, 'I don't know him,' I would be like you, a liar. But I know him, and keep his word. Your father Abraham rejoiced to see my day. He saw it, and was glad."

The Jews therefore said to him, "You are not yet fifty years old, and have you seen Abraham?"

Jesus said to them, "Most certainly, I tell you, before Abraham came into existence, I AM" (John 8:42-58).

138

"Most certainly, I tell you, one who doesn't enter by the door into the sheep fold, but climbs up some other way, the same is a thief and a robber. But one who enters in by the door is the shepherd of the sheep. The gatekeeper opens the gate for him, and the sheep listen to his voice. He calls his own sheep by name, and leads them out. Whenever he brings out his own sheep, he goes before them, and the sheep follow him, for they know his voice. They will by no means follow a stranger, but will flee from him; for they don't know the voice of strangers." Jesus spoke this parable to them, but they didn't understand what he was telling them.

Jesus therefore said to them again, "Most certainly, I tell you, I am the sheep's door. All who came before me are thieves and robbers, but the sheep didn't listen to them. I am the door. If anyone enters in by me, he will be saved, and will go in and go out, and will find pasture. The thief only comes to steal, kill, and destroy. I came that they may have life, and may have it abundantly. I am the good shepherd. The good shepherd lays down his life for the sheep. He who is a hired hand, and not a shepherd, who doesn't own the sheep, sees the wolf coming, leaves the sheep, and flees. The wolf snatches the sheep, and scatters them. The hired hand flees because he is a hired hand, and doesn't care for the sheep. I am the good shepherd. I know my own, and I'm known by my own; even as the Father knows me, and I know the Father. I lay down my life for the sheep. I have other sheep, which are not of this fold. I must bring them also, and they will hear my voice. They will become one flock with one shepherd. Therefore the Father loves me, because I lay down my life, that I may take it again. No one takes it away from me, but I lay it down by myself. I have power to lay it down, and I have power to take it again. I received this commandment from my Father" (John 10:1-18).

"I am the way, the truth, and the life. No one comes to the Father, except through me. If you had known me, you would have known my Father also. From now on, you know him, and have seen him."

Philip said to him, "Lord, show us the Father, and that will be enough for us."

Jesus said to him, "Have I been with you such a long time, and do you not know me, Philip? He who has seen me has seen the Father. How do you say, 'Show us the Father?' Don't you believe that I am in the Father, and the Father in me? The words that I tell you, I speak not from myself; but the Father who lives in me does his works. Believe me that I am in the Father, and the Father in me; or else believe me for the very works' sake" (John 14:6-11).

Lifting up his eyes to heaven, [Jesus] said, "Father, the time has come. Glorify your Son, that your Son may also glorify you; even as you gave him authority over all flesh, he will give eternal life to all whom you have given him. This is eternal life, that they should know you, the only true God, and him whom you sent, Jesus Christ. I glorified you on the earth. I have accomplished the work which you have given me to do. Now, Father, glorify me with your own self with the glory which I had with you before the world existed. I revealed your name to the people whom you have given me out of the world. They were yours, and you have given them to me. They have kept your word. Now they have known that all things whatever you have given me are from you, for the words which you have given me I have given to them, and they received them, and knew for sure that I came from you, and they have believed that you sent me" (John 17:1-8).

Judgment

"Don't judge, so that you won't be judged. For with whatever judgment you judge, you will be judged; and with whatever measure you measure, it will be measured to you. Why do you see the speck that is in your brother's eye, but don't consider the beam that is in your own eye? Or how will you tell your brother, 'Let me remove the speck from your eye;' and behold, the beam is in your own eye? You hypocrite! First remove the beam out of your own eye, and then you can see clearly to remove the speck out of your brother's eye" (Matthew 7:1-6, also Luke 6:37-38, 41-42).

"Either make the tree good, and its fruit good, or make the tree corrupt, and its fruit corrupt; for the tree is known by its fruit. You offspring of vipers, how can you, being evil, speak good things? For out of the abundance of the heart, the mouth speaks. The good man out of his good treasure brings out good things, and the evil man out of his evil treasure brings out evil things. I tell you that every idle word that men speak, they will give account of it in the day of judgment. For by your words you will be justified, and by your words you will be condemned" (Matthew 12:33-37, also Luke 6:43-45).

[See **Parable of Sheep and Goats** (Matthew 25:31-46).]

He also gave him authority to execute judgment, because he is a son of man. Don't marvel at this, for the hour comes, in which all that are in the tombs will hear his voice, and will come out; those who have done good, to the resurrection of life; and those who have done evil, to the resurrection of judgment. I can of myself do nothing. As I hear, I judge, and my judgment is righteous; because I don't seek my own will, but the will of my Father who sent me" (John 5:27-30).

Don't judge according to appearance, but judge righteous judgment" (John 7:24).

As he passed by, he saw a man blind from birth. His disciples asked him, "Rabbi, who sinned, this man or his parents, that he was born blind?"
Jesus answered, "Neither did this man sin, nor his parents; but, that the works of God might be revealed in him" (John 9:1-3).

[After Jesus healed the blind man, he asked], "Do you believe in the Son of God?"
He answered, "Who is he, Lord, that I may believe in him?"
Jesus said to him, "You have both seen him, and it is he who speaks with you."
He said, "Lord, I believe!" and he worshiped him.
Jesus said, "I came into this world for judgment, that those who don't see may see; and that those who see may become blind."
Those of the Pharisees who were with him heard these things, and said to him, "Are we also blind?"

Jesus said to them, "If you were blind, you would have no sin; but now you say, 'We see.' Therefore your sin remains" (John 9:35-41).

Kingdom of heaven

He set another parable before them, saying, "The Kingdom of Heaven is like a man who sowed good seed in his field, but while people slept, his enemy came and sowed darnel weeds also among the wheat, and went away. But when the blade sprang up and produced fruit, then the darnel weeds appeared also. The servants of the householder came and said to him, 'Sir, didn't you sow good seed in your field? Where did these darnel weeds come from?'

"He said to them, 'An enemy has done this.'

"The servants asked him, 'Do you want us to go and gather them up?'

"But he said, 'No, lest perhaps while you gather up the darnel weeds, you root up the wheat with them. Let both grow together until the harvest, and in the harvest time I will tell the reapers, "First, gather up the darnel weeds, and bind them in bundles to burn them; but gather the wheat into my barn."'"

He set another parable before them, saying, "The Kingdom of Heaven is like a grain of mustard seed, which a man took, and sowed in his field; which indeed is smaller than all seeds. But when it is grown, it is greater than the herbs, and becomes a tree, so that the birds of the air come and lodge in its branches."

He spoke another parable to them. "The Kingdom of Heaven is like yeast, which a woman took, and hid in three measures of meal, until it was all leavened (Matthew 13:24-33).

Then Jesus sent the multitudes away, and went into the house. His disciples came to him, saying, "Explain to us the parable of the darnel weeds of the field."

He answered them, "He who sows the good seed is the Son of Man, the field is the world; and the good seed, these are the children of the Kingdom; and the darnel weeds are the children of the evil one. The enemy who sowed them is the devil. The harvest is the end of the age, and the reapers are angels. As therefore the darnel weeds are gathered up and burned with fire; so will it be at the end of this age. The Son of Man will send out his angels, and they will gather out of his Kingdom all things that cause stumbling, and those who do iniquity, and will cast them into the furnace of fire. There will be weeping and the gnashing of teeth. Then the righteous will shine like the sun in the Kingdom of their Father. He who has ears to hear, let him hear.

"Again, the Kingdom of Heaven is like a treasure hidden in the field, which a man found, and hid. In his joy, he goes and sells all that he has, and buys that field.

"Again, the Kingdom of Heaven is like a man who is a merchant seeking fine pearls, who having found one pearl of great price, he went and sold all that he had, and bought it.

"Again, the Kingdom of Heaven is like a dragnet, that was cast into the sea, and gathered some fish of every kind, which, when it was filled, they drew up on the beach. They sat down, and gathered the good into containers, but the bad they threw away. So will it be in the end of the world. The angels will come and separate the wicked from among the righteous, and will cast them into the furnace of fire. There will be the weeping and the gnashing of teeth." Jesus said to them, "Have you understood all these things?"

They answered him, "Yes, Lord."

He said to them, "Therefore every scribe who has been made a disciple in the Kingdom of Heaven is like a man who is a householder, who brings out of his treasure new and old things" (Matthew 13:36-52).

Being asked by the Pharisees when God's Kingdom would come, he answered them, "God's Kingdom doesn't come with observation; neither will they say, 'Look, here!' or, 'Look, there!' for behold, God's Kingdom is within you" (Luke 17:20-21).

[See also **Parable of Feast in God's Kingdom** (Luke 14:15-24, also Matthew 22:1-10).]

The Last Days
(See End of the Age)

143

The Law

"Don't think that I came to destroy the law or the prophets. I didn't come to destroy, but to fulfill. For most certainly, I tell you, until heaven and earth pass away, not even one smallest letter or one tiny pen stroke shall in any way pass away from the law, until all things are accomplished. Whoever, therefore, shall break one of these least commandments, and teach others to do so, shall be called least in the Kingdom of Heaven; but whoever shall do and teach them shall be called great in the Kingdom of Heaven. For I tell you that unless your righteousness exceeds that of the scribes and Pharisees, there is no way you will enter into the Kingdom of Heaven" (Matthew 5:17-20).

He departed there, and went into their synagogue. And behold there was a man with a withered hand. They asked him, "Is it lawful to heal on the Sabbath day?" that they might accuse him.

He said to them, "What man is there among you, who has one sheep, and if this one falls into a pit on the Sabbath day, won't he grab on to it, and lift it out? Of how much more value then is a man than a sheep! Therefore it is lawful to do good on the Sabbath day." Then he told the man, "Stretch out your hand." He stretched it out; and it was restored whole, just like the other" (Matthew 12:9-13, also Mark 3:1-6, Luke 6:6-11).

Love

"But I tell you who hear: love your enemies, do good to those who hate you, bless those who curse you, and pray for those who mistreat you. To him who strikes you on the cheek, offer also the other; and from him who takes away your cloak, don't withhold your coat also. Give to everyone who asks you, and don't ask him who takes away your goods to give them back again.

"As you would like people to do to you, do exactly so to them. If you love those who love you, what credit is that to you? For even sinners love those who love them. If you do good to those who do good to you, what credit is that to you? For even sinners do the same. If you lend to those from whom you hope to receive, what credit is that to you? Even sinners lend to sinners, to receive back as much. But love your enemies, and do good, and lend, expecting nothing back; and your reward will be great, and you will be children of the Most High; for he is kind toward the unthankful and evil.

"Therefore be merciful, even as your Father is also merciful" (Luke 6:27-36, also Matthew 5:43-48).

One of them, a lawyer, asked him a question, testing him. "Teacher, which is the greatest commandment in the law?"

Jesus said to him, "'You shall love the Lord your God with all your heart, with all your soul, and with all your mind.' This is the first and great commandment. A second likewise is this, 'You shall love your neighbor as yourself.' The whole law and the prophets depend on these two commandments" (Matthew 22:35-40, also Luke 10:26-27).

"A new commandment I give to you, that you love one another. Just as I have loved you, you also love one another. By this everyone will know that you are my disciples, if you have love for one another" (John 13:34-35; also 15:12, 17).

"Greater love has no one than this, that someone lay down his life for his friends" (John 15:13).

Lust

"You have heard that it was said, 'You shall not commit adultery;' but I tell you that everyone who gazes at a woman to lust after her has committed adultery with her already in his heart" (Matthew 5:27-28).

Marriage

Pharisees came to him, testing him, and saying, "Is it lawful for a man to divorce his wife for any reason?"

He answered, "Haven't you read that he who made them from the beginning made them male and female, and said, 'For this cause a man shall leave his father and mother, and shall join to his wife; and the two shall become one flesh?' So that they are no more two, but one flesh. What therefore God has joined together, don't let man tear apart."

They asked him, "Why then did Moses command us to give her a bill of divorce, and divorce her?"

He said to them, "Moses, because of the hardness of your hearts, allowed you to divorce your wives, but from the beginning it has not been so. I tell you that whoever divorces his wife, except for sexual immorality, and marries another, commits adultery; and he who marries her when she is divorced commits adultery."

His disciples said to him, "If this is the case of the man with his wife, it is not expedient to marry."

But he said to them, "Not all men can receive this saying, but those to whom it is given. For there are eunuchs who were born that way from their mother's womb, and there are eunuchs who were made eunuchs by men; and there are eunuchs who made themselves eunuchs for the Kingdom of Heaven's sake. He who is able to receive it, let him receive it" (Matthew 19:3-12, also Mark 10:2-12).

Money

"No one can serve two masters, for either he will hate the one and love the other; or else he will be devoted to one and despise the other. You can't serve both God and Mammon" (Matthew 6:24, Luke 16:13).

[See **Parable of Rich Man** (Luke 12:14-20).]

Oaths
(See Vows)

Obedience

A man had two sons, and he came to the first, and said, 'Son, go work today in my vineyard.' He answered, 'I will not,' but afterward he changed his mind, and went. He came to the second, and said the same thing. He answered, 'I go, sir,' but he didn't go. Which of the two did the will of his father?"

They said to him, "The first."

146

Jesus said to them, "Most certainly I tell you that the tax collectors and the prostitutes are entering into God's Kingdom before you. For John came to you in the way of righteousness, and you didn't believe him, but the tax collectors and the prostitutes believed him. When you saw it, you didn't even repent afterward, that you might believe him (Matthew 21:28-32).

"Be like men watching for their lord, when he returns from the marriage feast; that, when he comes and knocks, they may immediately open to him. Blessed are those servants, whom the lord will find watching when he comes. Most certainly I tell you, that he will dress himself, and make them recline, and will come and serve them. They will be blessed if he comes in the second or third watch, and finds them so. But know this, that if the master of the house had known in what hour the thief was coming, he would have watched, and not allowed his house to be broken into. Therefore be ready also, for the Son of Man is coming in an hour that you don't expect him."

Peter said to him, "Lord, are you telling this parable to us, or to everybody?"

The Lord said, "Who then is the faithful and wise steward, whom his lord will set over his household, to give them their portion of food at the right times? Blessed is that servant whom his lord will find doing so when he comes. Truly I tell you, that he will set him over all that he has. But if that servant says in his heart, 'My lord delays his coming,' and begins to beat the menservants and the maidservants, and to eat and drink, and to be drunken, then the lord of that servant will come in a day when he isn't expecting him, and in an hour that he doesn't know, and will cut him in two, and place his portion with the unfaithful. That servant, who knew his lord's will, and didn't prepare, nor do what he wanted, will be beaten with many stripes, but he who didn't know, and did things worthy of stripes, will be beaten with few stripes. To whomever much is given, of him will much be required; and to whom much was entrusted, of him more will be asked" (Luke 12:35-48, Matthew 24:45-51).

"If you love me, keep my commandments" (John 14:15).

"One who has my commandments, and keeps them, that person is one who loves me. One who loves me will be loved by my Father, and I will love him, and will reveal myself to him."

"If a man loves me, he will keep my word. My Father will love him, and we will come to him, and make our home with him. He who doesn't love me doesn't keep my words. The word which you hear isn't mine, but the Father's who sent me" (John 14:21, 23-24).

Parables

The disciples came, and said to him, "Why do you speak to them in parables?"

He answered them, "To you it is given to know the mysteries of the Kingdom of Heaven, but it is not given to them. For whoever has, to him will be given, and he will have abundance, but whoever doesn't have, from him will be taken away even that which he has. Therefore I speak to them in parables, because seeing they don't see, and hearing, they don't hear, neither do they understand. In them the prophecy of Isaiah is fulfilled, which says,

'By hearing you will hear,
and will in no way understand;
Seeing you will see,
and will in no way perceive:
for this people's heart has grown callous,
their ears are dull of hearing,
they have closed their eyes;
or else perhaps they might perceive with their eyes,
hear with their ears,
understand with their heart,
and would turn again;
and I would heal them.'

"But blessed are your eyes, for they see; and your ears, for they hear. For most certainly I tell you that many prophets and righteous men desired to see the things which you see, and didn't see them; and to hear the things which you hear, and didn't hear them (Matthew 13:10-17, also Mark 4:10-12, Luke 8:9-10).

148

Jesus spoke all these things in parables to the multitudes; and without a parable, he didn't speak to them, that it might be fulfilled which was spoken through the prophet, saying,

"I will open my mouth in parables;
I will utter things hidden from the foundation of the world" (Matthew 13:34-35, also Mark 4:33-34).

Parable of Feast in God's Kingdom

When one of those who sat at the table with him heard these things, he said to him, "Blessed is he who will feast in God's Kingdom!" "A certain man made a great supper, and he invited many people. He sent out his servant at supper time to tell those who were invited, 'Come, for everything is ready now.' They all as one began to make excuses.

"The first said to him, 'I have bought a field, and I must go and see it. Please have me excused.'

"Another said, 'I have bought five yoke of oxen, and I must go try them out. Please have me excused.'

"Another said, 'I have married a wife, and therefore I can't come.'

"That servant came, and told his lord these things. Then the master of the house, being angry, said to his servant, 'Go out quickly into the streets and lanes of the city, and bring in the poor, maimed, blind, and lame.'

"The servant said, 'Lord, it is done as you commanded, and there is still room.'

"The lord said to the servant, 'Go out into the highways and hedges, and compel them to come in, that my house may be filled. For I tell you that none of those men who were invited will taste of my supper'" (Luke 14:15-24, also Matthew 22:1-14).

Parable of Good Samaritan

Jesus answered, "A certain man was going down from Jerusalem to Jericho, and he fell among robbers, who both stripped him and beat him, and departed, leaving him half dead. By chance a certain priest was going down that way. When he saw him, he passed by on the other side. In the same way a Levite also, when he came to the place, and saw him, passed by on the other side. But a certain Samaritan, as he traveled, came where he was. When he saw him, he was moved with compassion, came to him, and bound up his wounds, pouring on oil and wine. He set him on his own animal, and brought him to an inn, and took care of him. On the next day, when he departed, he took out two [coins, each worth a day's wage], and gave them to the host, and said to him, 'Take care of him. Whatever you spend beyond that, I will repay you when I return.' Now which of these three do you think seemed to be a neighbor to him who fell among the robbers?"

He said, "He who showed mercy on him."

Then Jesus said to him, "Go and do likewise" (Luke 10:30-37).

Parable of Sheep and Goats

"But when the Son of Man comes in his glory, and all the holy angels with him, then he will sit on the throne of his glory. Before him all the nations will be gathered, and he will separate them one from another, as a shepherd separates the sheep from the goats. He will set the sheep on his right hand, but the goats on the left. Then the King will tell those on his right hand, 'Come, blessed of my Father, inherit the Kingdom prepared for you from the foundation of the world; for I was hungry, and you gave me food to eat. I was thirsty, and you gave me drink. I was a stranger, and you took me in. I was naked, and you clothed me. I was sick, and you visited me. I was in prison, and you came to me.'

"Then the righteous will answer him, saying, 'Lord, when did we see you hungry, and feed you; or thirsty, and give you a drink? When did we see you as a stranger, and take you in; or naked, and clothe you? When did we see you sick, or in prison, and come to you?'

"The King will answer them, 'Most certainly I tell you, because you did it to one of the least of these my brothers , you did it to me.' Then he will say also to those on the left hand, 'Depart from me, you cursed, into the eternal fire which is prepared for the devil and his angels; for I was hungry, and you didn't give me food to eat; I was thirsty, and you gave me no drink; I was a stranger, and you didn't take me in; naked, and you didn't clothe me; sick, and in prison, and you didn't visit me.'

"Then they will also answer, saying, 'Lord, when did we see you hungry, or thirsty, or a stranger, or naked, or sick, or in prison, and didn't help you?'

"Then he will answer them, saying, 'Most certainly I tell you, because you didn't do it to one of the least of these, you didn't do it to me.' These will go away into eternal punishment, but the righteous into eternal life" (Matthew 25:31-46).

Parable of Rewards

"For the Kingdom of Heaven is like a man who was the master of a household, who went out early in the morning to hire laborers for his vineyard. When he had agreed with the laborers for a [silver coin] a day, he sent them into his vineyard. He went out about the third hour, and saw others standing idle in the marketplace. He said to them, 'You also go into the vineyard, and whatever is right I will give you.' So they went their way. Again he went out about the sixth and the ninth hour, and did likewise. About the eleventh hour he went out, and found others standing idle. He said to them, 'Why do you stand here all day idle?'

"They said to him, 'Because no one has hired us.'

"He said to them, 'You also go into the vineyard, and you will receive whatever is right.' When evening had come, the lord of the vineyard said to his manager, 'Call the laborers and pay them their wages, beginning from the last to the first.'

"When those who were hired at about the eleventh hour came, they each received [one silver coin]. When the first came, they supposed that they would receive more; and they likewise each received [one silver coin]. When they received it, they murmured against the master of the household, saying, 'These last have spent one hour, and you have made them equal to us, who have borne the burden of the day and the scorching heat!'

"But he answered one of them, 'Friend, I am doing you no wrong. Didn't you agree with me for [one silver coin]? Take that which is yours, and go your way. It is my desire to give to this last just as much as to you. Isn't it lawful for me to do what I want to with what I own? Or is your eye evil, because I am good?' So the last will be first, and the first last. For many are called, but few are chosen" (Matthew 20:1-16).

Parable of Rich Man

"Beware! Keep yourselves from covetousness, for a man's life doesn't consist of the abundance of the things which he possesses."

He spoke a parable to them, saying, "The ground of a certain rich man produced abundantly. He reasoned within himself, saying, 'What will I do, because I don't have room to store my crops?' He said, 'This is what I will do. I will pull down my barns, and build bigger ones, and there I will store all my grain and my goods. I will tell my soul, "Soul, you have many goods laid up for many years. Take your ease, eat, drink, be merry."'

"But God said to him, 'You foolish one, tonight your soul is required of you. The things which you have prepared—whose will they be?' So is he who lays up treasure for himself, and is not rich toward God" (Luke 12:15-21).

Parable of the Unforgiving Servant

Peter came and said to him, "Lord, how often shall my brother sin against me, and I forgive him? Until seven times?"

Jesus said to him, "I don't tell you until seven times, but, until seventy times seven.

"Therefore the Kingdom of Heaven is like a certain king, who wanted to reconcile accounts with his servants. When he had begun to reconcile, one was brought to him who owed him ten thousand talents. But because he couldn't pay, his lord commanded him to be sold, with his wife, his children, and all that he had, and payment to be made. The servant therefore fell down and knelt before him, saying, 'Lord, have patience with me, and I will repay you all!' The lord of that servant, being moved with compassion, released him, and forgave him the debt.

"But that servant went out, and found one of his fellow servants, who owed him one hundred [day's wages], and he grabbed him, and took him by the throat, saying, 'Pay me what you owe!'

"So his fellow servant fell down at his feet and begged him, saying, 'Have patience with me, and I will repay you!' He would not, but went and cast him into prison, until he should pay back that which was due. So when his fellow servants saw what was done, they were exceedingly sorry, and came and told to their lord all that was done. Then his lord called him in, and said to him, 'You wicked servant! I forgave you all that debt, because you begged me. Shouldn't you also have had mercy on your fellow servant, even as I had mercy on you?' His lord was angry, and delivered him to the tormentors, until he should pay all that was due to him. So my heavenly Father will also do to you, if you don't each forgive your brother from your hearts for his misdeeds" (Matthew 18:21-35).

Parable of the Vineyard

He began to tell the people this parable. "A man planted a vineyard, and rented it out to some farmers, and went into another country for a long time. At the proper season, he sent a servant to the farmers to collect his share of the fruit of the vineyard. But the farmers beat him, and sent him away empty. He sent yet another servant, and they also beat him, and treated him shamefully, and sent him away empty. He sent yet a third, and they also wounded him, and threw him out. The lord of the vineyard said, 'What shall I do? I will send my beloved son. It may be that seeing him, they will respect him.'

"But when the farmers saw him, they reasoned among themselves, saying, 'This is the heir. Come, let's kill him, that the inheritance may be ours.' They threw him out of the vineyard, and killed him. What therefore will the lord of the vineyard do to them? He will come and destroy these farmers, and will give the vineyard to others."

When they heard it, they said, "May it never be!"

But he looked at them, and said, "Then what is this that is written,

'The stone which the builders rejected,
the same was made the chief cornerstone?'
Everyone who falls on that stone will be broken to

pieces,

but it will crush whomever it falls on to dust" (Luke
20:9-18, also Matthew 21:33-44, Mark 12:1-11).

Peace

Peace I leave with you. My peace I give to you; not as the world
gives, give I to you. Don't let your heart be troubled, neither let it be
fearful" (John 14:27).

Persecution

"Blessed are those who have been persecuted for righteousness'
sake,

for theirs is the Kingdom of Heaven.

"Blessed are you when people reproach you, persecute you, and
say all kinds of evil against you falsely, for my sake. Rejoice, and be
exceedingly glad, for great is your reward in heaven. For that is how
they persecuted the prophets who were before you (Matthew 5:10-
12, also Luke 6:22-23).

"Behold, I send you out as sheep among wolves. Therefore be
wise as serpents, and harmless as doves. But beware of men: for they
will deliver you up to councils, and in their synagogues they will
scourge you. Yes, and you will be brought before governors and
kings for my sake, for a testimony to them and to the nations. But
when they deliver you up, don't be anxious how or what you will
say, for it will be given you in that hour what you will say. For it is
not you who speak, but the Spirit of your Father who speaks in you.

"Brother will deliver up brother to death, and the father his child.
Children will rise up against parents, and cause them to be put to
death. You will be hated by all men for my name's sake, but he who
endures to the end will be saved. But when they persecute you in this
city, flee into the next, for most certainly I tell you, you will not have
gone through the cities of Israel, until the Son of Man has come.

"A disciple is not above his teacher, nor a servant above his lord.
It is enough for the disciple that he be like his teacher, and the
servant like his lord. If they have called the master of the house
Beelzebul, how much more those of his household! Therefore don't

be afraid of them, for there is nothing covered that will not be revealed; and hidden that will not be known. What I tell you in the darkness, speak in the light; and what you hear whispered in the ear, proclaim on the housetops. Don't be afraid of those who kill the body, but are not able to kill the soul. Rather, fear him who is able to destroy both soul and body in Gehenna (Matthew 10:16-28).

"Don't think that I came to send peace on the earth. I didn't come to send peace, but a sword. For I came to set a man at odds against his father, and a daughter against her mother, and a daughter-in-law against her mother-in-law. A man's foes will be those of his own household. He who loves father or mother more than me is not worthy of me; and he who loves son or daughter more than me isn't worthy of me. He who doesn't take his cross and follow after me, isn't worthy of me. He who seeks his life will lose it; and he who loses his life for my sake will find it. He who receives you receives me, and he who receives me receives him who sent me" (Matthew 10:34-40, also Luke 12:51-53, 14:26-27).

"If the world hates you, you know that it has hated me before it hated you. If you were of the world, the world would love its own. But because you are not of the world, since I chose you out of the world, therefore the world hates you. Remember the word that I said to you: 'A servant is not greater than his lord.' If they persecuted me, they will also persecute you. If they kept my word, they will keep yours also. But all these things will they do to you for my name's sake, because they don't know him who sent me. If I had not come and spoken to them, they would not have had sin; but now they have no excuse for their sin. He who hates me, hates my Father also. If I hadn't done among them the works which no one else did, they wouldn't have had sin. But now have they seen and also hated both me and my Father. But this happened so that the word may be fulfilled which was written in their law, 'They hated me without a cause'" (John 15:18-25).

"These things have I spoken to you, so that you wouldn't be caused to stumble. They will put you out of the synagogues. Yes, the time comes that whoever kills you will think that he offers service to God. They will do these things because they have not known the Father, nor me. But I have told you these things, so that when the time comes, you may remember that I told you about them. I didn't tell you these things from the beginning, because I was with you." (John 16:1-4).

Prayer

"When you pray, you shall not be as the hypocrites, for they love to stand and pray in the synagogues and in the corners of the streets, that they may be seen by men. Most certainly, I tell you, they have received their reward. But you, when you pray, enter into your inner room, and having shut your door, pray to your Father who is in secret, and your Father who sees in secret will reward you openly. In praying, don't use vain repetitions, as the Gentiles do; for they think that they will be heard for their much speaking. Therefore don't be like them, for your Father knows what things you need, before you ask him. Pray like this: 'Our Father in heaven, may your name be kept holy. Let your Kingdom come. Let your will be done, as in heaven, so on earth. Give us today our daily bread. Forgive us our debts, as we also forgive our debtors. Bring us not into temptation, but deliver us from the evil one. For yours is the Kingdom, the power, and the glory forever. Amen'" (Matthew 6:5-13, also Luke 11:2-4).

"Ask, and it will be given you. Seek, and you will find. Knock, and it will be opened for you. For everyone who asks receives. He who seeks finds. To him who knocks it will be opened. Or who is there among you, who, if his son asks him for bread, will give him a stone? Or if he asks for a fish, who will give him a serpent? [11] If you then, being evil, know how to give good gifts to your children, how much more will your Father who is in heaven give good things to those who ask him!" (Matthew 7:7-11 also Luke 11:9-13).

"Again, assuredly I tell you, that if two of you will agree on earth concerning anything that they will ask, it will be done for them by my Father who is in heaven" (Matthew 18:19).

"Therefore I tell you, all things whatever you pray and ask for, believe that you have received them, and you shall have them" (Mark 11:24).

He also spoke a parable to them that they must always pray, and not give up, saying, "There was a judge in a certain city who didn't fear God, and didn't respect man. A widow was in that city, and she often came to him, saying, 'Defend me from my adversary!' He wouldn't for a while, but afterward he said to himself, 'Though I neither fear God, nor respect man, yet because this widow bothers me, I will defend her, or else she will wear me out by her continual coming.'"

The Lord said, "Listen to what the unrighteous judge says. Won't God avenge his chosen ones, who are crying out to him day and night, and yet he exercises patience with them? I tell you that he will avenge them quickly. Nevertheless, when the Son of Man comes, will he find faith on the earth?" (Luke 18:1-8).

"Most certainly I tell you, he who believes in me, the works that I do, he will do also; and he will do greater works than these, because I am going to my Father. Whatever you will ask in my name, that will I do, that the Father may be glorified in the Son. If you will ask anything in my name, I will do it" (John 14:12-14).

Reconciliation

"If therefore you are offering your gift at the altar, and there remember that your brother has anything against you, leave your gift there before the altar, and go your way. First be reconciled to your brother, and then come and offer your gift. Agree with your adversary quickly, while you are with him on the way; lest perhaps the prosecutor deliver you to the judge, and the judge deliver you to the officer, and you be cast into prison. Most certainly I tell you, you shall by no means get out of there, until you have paid the last penny" (Matthew 5:23-26, also Luke 12:57-59).

Rest

"Come to me, all you who labor and are heavily burdened, and I will give you rest. Take my yoke upon you, and learn from me, for I am gentle and humble in heart; and you will find rest for your souls. For my yoke is easy, and my burden is light" (Matthew 11:28-30).

Riches

Behold, one came to him and said, "Good teacher, what good thing shall I do, that I may have eternal life?"

He said to him, "Why do you call me good? No one is good but one, that is, God. But if you want to enter into life, keep the commandments."

He said to him, "Which ones?"

Jesus said, "'You shall not murder.' 'You shall not commit adultery.' 'You shall not steal.' 'You shall not offer false testimony.' 'Honor your father and mother.' And, 'You shall love your neighbor as yourself.'"

The young man said to him, "All these things I have observed from my youth. What do I still lack?"

Jesus said to him, "If you want to be perfect, go, sell what you have, and give to the poor, and you will have treasure in heaven; and come, follow me." But when the young man heard the saying, he went away sad, for he was one who had great possessions. Jesus said to his disciples, "Most certainly I say to you, a rich man will enter into the Kingdom of Heaven with difficulty. Again I tell you, it is easier for a camel to go through a needle's eye, than for a rich man to enter into God's Kingdom."

When the disciples heard it, they were exceedingly astonished, saying, "Who then can be saved?"

Looking at them, Jesus said, "With men this is impossible, but with God all things are possible" (Matthew 19:16-26, also Mark 10:17-31, Luke 18:18-30).

Second Coming of Jesus

"Then the Kingdom of Heaven will be like ten virgins, who took their lamps, and went out to meet the bridegroom. Five of them were foolish, and five were wise. Those who were foolish, when they took their lamps, took no oil with them, but the wise took oil in their vessels with their lamps. Now while the bridegroom delayed, they all slumbered and slept. But at midnight there was a cry, 'Behold! The bridegroom is coming! Come out to meet him!' Then all those virgins arose, and trimmed their lamps. The foolish said to the wise, 'Give us some of your oil, for our lamps are going out.' But the wise answered, saying, 'What if there isn't enough for us and you? You go rather to those who sell, and buy for yourselves.' While they went away to buy, the bridegroom came, and those who were ready went in with him to the marriage feast, and the door was shut. Afterward the other virgins also came, saying, 'Lord, Lord, open to us.' But he answered, 'Most certainly I tell you, I don't know you.' Watch therefore, for you don't know the day nor the hour in which the Son of Man is coming (Matthew 25:1-13).

[See also **End of the Age**.]

Servanthood

But who is there among you, having a servant plowing or keeping sheep, that will say, when he comes in from the field, 'Come immediately and sit down at the table,' and will not rather tell him, 'Prepare my supper, clothe yourself properly, and serve me, while I eat and drink. Afterward you shall eat and drink'? Does he thank that servant because he did the things that were commanded? I think not. Even so you also, when you have done all the things that are commanded you, say, 'We are unworthy servants. We have done our duty'" (Luke 17:7-10).

The sick

"Those who are healthy have no need for a physician, but those who are sick. I came not to call the righteous, but sinners to repentance" (Mark 2:17, also Matthew 9:12, Luke 5:31-32).

Stewardship

"For it is like a man, going into another country, who called his own servants, and entrusted his goods to them. To one he gave five talents, to another two, to another one; to each according to his own ability. [See value of "talent" in Glossary.] Then he went on his journey. Immediately he who received the five talents went and traded with them, and made another five talents. In the same way, he also who got the two gained another two. But he who received the one talent went away and dug in the earth, and hid his lord's money.

"Now after a long time the lord of those servants came, and reconciled accounts with them. He who received the five talents came and brought another five talents, saying, 'Lord, you delivered to me five talents. Behold, I have gained another five talents besides them.'

"His lord said to him, 'Well done, good and faithful servant. You have been faithful over a few things, I will set you over many things. Enter into the joy of your lord.'

"He also who got the two talents came and said, 'Lord, you delivered to me two talents. Behold, I have gained another two talents besides them.'

"His lord said to him, 'Well done, good and faithful servant. You have been faithful over a few things, I will set you over many things. Enter into the joy of your lord.'

"He also who had received the one talent came and said, 'Lord, I knew you that you are a hard man, reaping where you did not sow, and gathering where you did not scatter. I was afraid, and went away and hid your talent in the earth. Behold, you have what is yours.'

"But his lord answered him, 'You wicked and slothful servant. You knew that I reap where I didn't sow, and gather where I didn't scatter. You ought therefore to have deposited my money with the bankers, and at my coming I should have received back my own with interest. Take away therefore the talent from him, and give it to him who has the ten talents. For to everyone who has will be given, and he will have abundance, but from him who doesn't have, even that which he has will be taken away. Throw out the unprofitable servant into the outer darkness, where there will be weeping and gnashing of teeth'" (Matthew 25:14-30, also Luke 19:11-27).

Taxes

Then the Pharisees went and took counsel how they might entrap [Jesus] in his talk. They sent their disciples to him, along with the

Herodians, saying, "Teacher, we know that you are honest, and teach the way of God in truth, no matter whom you teach, for you aren't partial to anyone. Tell us therefore, what do you think? Is it lawful to pay taxes to Caesar, or not?"

But Jesus perceived their wickedness, and said, "Why do you test me, you hypocrites? Show me the tax money."

They brought to him a denarius.

He asked them, "Whose is this image and inscription?"

They said to him, "Caesar's."

Then he said to them, "Give therefore to Caesar the things that are Caesar's, and to God the things that are God's" (Matthew 22:15-21, also Luke 20:21-25).

Temptation

"Woe to the world because of occasions of stumbling! For it must be that the occasions come, but woe to that person through whom the occasion comes! If your hand or your foot causes you to stumble, cut it off, and cast it from you. It is better for you to enter into life maimed or crippled, rather than having two hands or two feet to be cast into the eternal fire. If your eye causes you to stumble, pluck it out, and cast it from you. It is better for you to enter into life with one eye, rather than having two eyes to be cast into the Gehenna of fire" (Matthew 16:7-9, also Mark 9:42-48, Luke 17:1-3).

Tradition

He also told a parable to them. "No one puts a piece from a new garment on an old garment, or else he will tear the new, and also the piece from the new will not match the old. No one puts new wine into old wine skins, or else the new wine will burst the skins, and it will be spilled, and the skins will be destroyed. But new wine must be put into fresh wine skins, and both are preserved. No man having drunk old wine immediately desires new, for he says, 'The old is better'" (Luke 5:36-39, also Mark 2:21-22).

Treasures

"Don't lay up treasures for yourselves on the earth, where moth and rust consume, and where thieves break through and steal; but lay up for yourselves treasures in heaven, where neither moth nor rust consume, and where thieves don't break through and steal; for where your treasure is, there your heart will be also" (Matthew 6:19-21, also Luke 12:33-34).

[See also **Riches**]

Vision
"The lamp of the body is the eye. If therefore your eye is sound, your whole body will be full of light. But if your eye is evil, your whole body will be full of darkness. If therefore the light that is in you is darkness, how great is the darkness!" (Matthew 6:22-23, also Luke 11:34-36).

Vows
"Again you have heard that it was said to them of old time, 'You shall not make false vows, but shall perform to the Lord your vows,' but I tell you, don't swear at all: neither by heaven, for it is the throne of God; nor by the earth, for it is the footstool of his feet; nor by Jerusalem, for it is the city of the great King. Neither shall you swear by your head, for you can't make one hair white or black. But let your 'Yes' be 'Yes' and your 'No' be 'No.' Whatever is more than these is of the evil one" (Matthew 5:33-37).

Witnessing
"You are the salt of the earth, but if the salt has lost its flavor, with what will it be salted? It is then good for nothing, but to be cast out and trodden under the feet of men. You are the light of the world. A city located on a hill can't be hidden. Neither do you light a lamp, and put it under a measuring basket, but on a stand; and it shines to all who are in the house. Even so, let your light shine before men; that they may see your good works, and glorify your Father who is in heaven" (Matthew 5:13-16, also Mark 9:50, Luke 14:34-35).

Jesus said to them, "My food is to do the will of him who sent me, and to accomplish his work. Don't you say, 'There are yet four months until the harvest?' Behold, I tell you, lift up your eyes, and look at the fields, that they are white for harvest already. He who reaps receives wages, and gathers fruit to eternal life; that both he who sows and he who reaps may rejoice together. For in this the saying is true, 'One sows, and another reaps.' I sent you to reap that for which you haven't labored. Others have labored, and you have entered into their labor" (John 4:34-38).

Word of God

"Everyone therefore who hears these words of mine, and does them, I will liken him to a wise man, who built his house on a rock. The rain came down, the floods came, and the winds blew, and beat on that house; and it didn't fall, for it was founded on the rock. Everyone who hears these words of mine, and doesn't do them will be like a foolish man, who built his house on the sand. The rain came down, the floods came, and the winds blew, and beat on that house; and it fell—and great was its fall" (Matthew 7:24-27, also Luke 6:46-49).

He spoke to them many things in parables, saying, "Behold, a farmer went out to sow. As he sowed, some seeds fell by the roadside, and the birds came and devoured them. Others fell on rocky ground, where they didn't have much soil, and immediately they sprang up, because they had no depth of earth. When the sun had risen, they were scorched. Because they had no root, they withered away. Others fell among thorns. The thorns grew up and choked them. Others fell on good soil, and yielded fruit: some one hundred times as much, some sixty, and some thirty. He who has ears to hear, let him hear."

"Hear, then, the parable of the farmer. When anyone hears the word of the Kingdom, and doesn't understand it, the evil one comes, and snatches away that which has been sown in his heart. This is what was sown by the roadside. What was sown on the rocky places, this is he who hears the word, and immediately with joy receives it; yet he has no root in himself, but endures for a while. When oppression or persecution arises because of the word, immediately he stumbles. What was sown among the thorns, this is he who hears

163

the word, but the cares of this age and the deceitfulness of riches choke the word, and he becomes unfruitful. What was sown on the good ground, this is he who hears the word, and understands it, who most certainly bears fruit, and produces, some one hundred times as much, some sixty, and some thirty (Matthew 13:3-9, 18-23; also Mark 4:1-9, 13-20; Luke 8:4-8, 11-15).

It came to pass, as he said these things, a certain woman out of the multitude lifted up her voice, and said to him, "Blessed is the womb that bore you, and the breasts which nursed you!"
But he said, "On the contrary, blessed are those who hear the word of God, and keep it" (Luke 11:27-28).

Jesus therefore said to those Jews who had believed him, "If you remain in my word, then you are truly my disciples. You will know the truth, and the truth will make you free" (John 8:31-32).

Worry
(See Anxiety)

Worship
The [Samaritan] woman said to him, "Sir, I perceive that you are a prophet. Our fathers worshiped in this mountain, and you Jews say that in Jerusalem is the place where people ought to worship."
Jesus said to her, "Woman, believe me, the hour comes, when neither in this mountain, nor in Jerusalem, will you worship the Father. You worship that which you don't know. We worship that which we know; for salvation is from the Jews. But the hour comes, and now is, when the true worshipers will worship the Father in spirit and truth, for the Father seeks such to be his worshipers. God is spirit, and those who worship him must worship in spirit and truth" (John 4:19-24).

Notes

As mentioned in the Introduction, the task of creating a chronological narrative of Jesus' life and a topical arrangement of his lessons is a bit like trying to create one giant jigsaw puzzle picture from four smaller jigsaw puzzle pictures. The subject is common to all four gospels—the life and lessons of Jesus—but the individual pieces from his followers, Matthew, Mark, Luke, and John, don't always fit snuggly together on one plane. Some stack on top of each other, others sideways, creating a three-dimensional picture. And John concludes his gospel by mentioning there are many missing pieces in the written record of Jesus' life. But ultimately, the pieces we have provide a consistent, multi-dimensional picture of Jesus.

The approach to Jesus' life

Many scholars, including early theologian Augustine (354-430) and reformer John Calvin (1509-1564), have attempted to arrange the story of Jesus chronologically, beginning with the announcement of his birth through his ascension back into heaven. (Calvin used only the first three gospels—Matthew, Mark, and Luke—to attempt a single, seamless—and one dimensional—narrative of Jesus' life.)

The challenges to this task include both a Hebrew and Hellenistic literary device of the first century of organizing stories by themes, rather than a strict chronology. These differences in order of events between gospel writers are not the result of reporting errors, but reflect the differences of theme and emphasis of the inspired writers. Many scholars argue that Mark is the most chronological of the gospels, perhaps using the apostle Peter as a source. Matthew and Luke tend to follow Mark's chronology. But John is more concerned with theological themes than with a linear order of events.

Augustine noted in his book, *Harmony of the Gospels*, the variations were also based on the roles of Jesus emphasized by each writer: Matthew on royalty, Mark on humanity, Luke on priesthood and John on divinity.

Another challenge is that Jesus spent three years in public ministry speaking to many different audiences in different settings. For instance, his famous "Beatitudes" are slightly different in Matthew 5 and Luke 6. Like any good speaker, Jesus probably adapted his messages to his audience. Matthew's account is introduced by "he went up onto the *mountain*. When he had sat down, his disciples came to him." Luke's records that Jesus "stood on *a level place*, with a crowd of his disciples *and* a great number of the people from all Judea and Jerusalem." (Or was it a level place *on* the mountain?) Critics point to the differences as a contradiction, not taking into consideration these may be different messages to different audiences in different settings.

In the sixteenth century, scholars devised another approach creating a parallel "harmony" with the gospels side by side in four columns rather than attempting a single, seamless story. Each gospel is fully inspired of God, but the literary styles of the gospel can't be forced into an arbitrary order. It is a three-dimensional jigsaw puzzle with the picture on both sides!

So, I've chosen to create a *general* chronology—using Mark's order, when the order differs between gospel writers—and have included references to complementary passages. The purpose is not to create a definitive work—that has been found to be impossible over the past two thousand years—but to give a feel for general trajectory of Jesus' life, death, and resurrection.

The approach to Jesus' lessons

I've have attempted to organize Jesus' teachings by the actual words of the gospel text. For instance, Jesus speaks specifically about "anxiety" rather than worry. So, I have used topic headings derived directly from the text. Where different gospels overlap, I've used the one with the most detail and then provided references to the other gospel's treatment of the topic.

And I've tried to use non-theological terms choosing John's "born anew" rather than saved or born again, "eternal life" rather than salvation, and so on.

Again, the intent is not an academic theology, but to make the teachings of Jesus accessible to believers and seekers as well.

The Bible version
The past fifty years have produced many reliable translations based on discoveries of ancient texts that pre-date the manuscripts used in the 1611 Authorized (King James Version). For instance, the Dead Sea Scrolls, discovered between 1946 and 1956 pre-date Jesus by approximately seventy years. They are significant because they include the earliest known surviving manuscripts of the Hebrew Bible and have guided new, more accurate translations of the Old Testament.

The rights to publish these new, more accurate translations are administered by major publishing house that have exclusive use of the particular translations. So, I have chosen to use *The World English* Bible, which was created as a public domain work that is copyright-free meaning that anyone may freely copy it in any form, including electronic and print formats.

The translation is based on the popular *American Standard Version of the Holy Bible* produced by fifty evangelical scholars and first published in 1901. The *WEB* translators include Baptist, Methodist, Pentecostal, Catholic, Anglican, Lutheran, non-denominational, and many more Christian groups. This broad representation helps guard against introducing sectarian bias into the work. In addition, the novel technique of publishing draft copies of the World English Bible on the Internet provides additional protection against bias, because all serious comments are carefully considered and the wording compared to the original language.

Ten percent of all profits from *Jesus: His Life and Lessons* goes to the WEB's publisher:

World Outreach Ministries
PO Box B
Marietta, GA 30061-0379

Glossary

Amen

"So be it" or "it is certainly so."

Angel

Literally means "messenger" or "envoy," usually refers to spiritual beings who normally are invisible to us, but can also appear as powerful humans.

Apostle

A delegate, messenger, or one sent forth with orders. In the gospels, it refers Jesus' inner circle of twelve followers named in Matthew 10:1-4, Luke 6:12-16, and Mark 3:13-19.

Baptize

To immerse in or wash with something. Often associated with water, but the New Testament includes baptism in the Holy Spirit, fire, the Body of Christ, and suffering. Baptism is a sign of repentance, as practiced by John the Baptizer, and of faith in Jesus Christ, as practiced by Jesus' disciples.

Beelzebul

A name for the devil which literally means "Lord of the Flies."

Behold

Outdated word for "take notice," "look at this."

Christ

The name is transcribed from the Greek word *Christos*, which is a translation of the Hebrew word *machiach*, meaning "messiah" or "anointed one." In Hebrew culture, a Messiah was a savior or liberator. When used with Jesus, it announces that he is the Savior of the world.

Crucify
Crucify means to execute someone by nailing them to a cross with metal spikes. Their hands are stretched out on the crossbeam with spikes driven through their wrists or hands. Their feet or ankles are attached to a cross with a metal spike. Roman crucifixion was generally done totally naked to maximize both shame and discomfort. Eventually, the pain, weakness, dehydration, and exhaustion from trying to breathe caused the victim to suffocate—but only after a prolonged struggle that sometimes lasted days.

Darnel
A weed grass that looks very much like wheat until it is mature and reveals it has black kernels of grain. Darnel was used as cheap feed for livestock, not for humans.

Demons
The one-third of angels in heaven, who rebelled against God and now inhabit the spiritual realms of earth under Satan's command.

Devil
The word "devil" comes from the Greek *diabolos*, which means "one prone to slander; a liar." Devil is used to refer to a fallen angel, also called "Satan."

Dispersion
Throughout the Old and New Testament, the Jewish people were "dispersed" or scattered into foreign countries. Abraham's descendents went to Egypt to secure food during a massive famine. Later Jews entered the land of Palestine in the Exodus, but later were taken into Babylonian captivity. The dispersion noted in John 7 probably referred to Jews who had moved to Greece for business opportunities.

Frankincense

An aromatic resin with a sweet, balsamic smell obtained from the trees of the Boswellia genus.

Gehenna

One of the words for hell comes from the Hebrew *Gey-Hinnom*, literally "Valley of Hinnom." This word originated as the name for a place south of the old city of Jerusalem where the city's rubbish was burned and babies burned alive as a sacrifice to pagan gods. Also used as a dumping ground for diseased animals and executed criminals.

Gospel

Gospel means "good news" or "glad tidings," specifically the Good News of Jesus' life, death, and resurrection for our salvation, healing, provision, and eternal life.

Hades

The concept of Hades was similar to the Old Testaments *sheol.* It was simply the place of the dead—often translated "the grave"—and not necessarily synonymous with hell (see below.)

Hell

A place of eternal punishment and torment.

Hypocrite

A stage actor; one who pretends to be someone other than who he or she is; a pretender.

I AM

When Moses was called from the burning bush to liberate Israel, he asked, "Behold, when I come to the children of Israel, and tell them, 'The God of your fathers has sent me to you;' and they ask me, 'What is his name?' What should I tell them?" God's answers, "You shall tell the children of Israel this: 'I AM has sent me to you.'" (Exodus 3:13-14).

Jesus identifies himself as I AM in John 8:42-58.

Jesus

"Jesus" is Greek for the Hebrew name *Yeshua*, which means "He will save."

Messiah

(See Christ)

Myrrh

Myrrh is the fragrant substance that oozes out of the stems and branches of the shrub/tree native to the Arabian deserts and parts of Africa. Myrrh was highly valued as a perfume and as an ingredient in medicinal and ceremonial ointments.

Nard

Also called "spikenard," the flowering plant grows in Nepal, China, and India. It is used in the manufacture of an intensely aromatic amber-colored oil. Since ancient times, it has been used as a perfume and as a medicine.

Pharisee

This Jewish sect was extremely legalistic in observing the written Law of Moses, but also created hundreds of man-made laws based on its interpretations of the Law. They differed with the Sadducees who observed only the written laws of Moses and didn't believe in the resurrection of the dead.

Praetorium

The Roman governor's residence and office building, and those who work there.

Priests

These members of the Jewish tribe of Levite served in the Temple and performed the rituals of sacrificing of animals to obtain forgiveness of personal and national sins.

Rabbi

A transliteration of the Hebrew word for "my teacher," used as a title of respect for Jewish teachers.

Rabboni

A transliteration of the Hebrew word for "great teacher."

Raca

Aramaic word which literally means "empty one," but implied empty-headed or foolish.

Repent

To change one's mind; turn away from sin and turn towards God; to reject one's past sins and determine to follow God.

Rue

An oriental plant (Ruta graveolens), having a strong, heavy odor and a bitter taste, used in medicine.

Sabbath

The seventh day of the week, set aside by God for his people to rest.

Saints

The Greek word for saints literally means "holy ones." Saints are people set apart for service to God as holy and separate, living in righteousness. Used in the Bible to refer to all Christians and to all of those who worship Yahweh in Old Testament times.

Sadducees

This group included the Jewish priests who maintained the Temple, as well as the wealthy aristocrats and ruling class. They observed only the written Law given to Moses, putting them at odds with the Pharisees and their hundreds of man-made rules deriving from the original Law. They did not believe in the resurrection of the dead or angels.

Samaritan

A resident of Samaria. The Samaritans and the Jews generally detested each other during the time that Jesus walked the Earth.

Satan

Satan means "accuser." This is one name for the devil, an enemy of God and God's people.

Scribe

One who copied God's law; often respected as teachers and authorities on God's law.

Sin

Any action or attitude that is not motivated by love for God or humanity (Matthew 22:36-40).

Soul

The emotions and intellect of a living person, as well as that person's very life. It is distinguished in the Bible from a person's spirit and body (1 Thessalonians 5:23, Hebrews 4:12).

Spirit

Spirit, breath, and wind all derive from the same Hebrew and Greek words. A person's spirit is the very essence of that person's life, which comes from God, who is a Spirit being (John 4:24, Genesis 1:2; 2:7). The Bible distinguishes between a person's spirit, soul, and body (1 Thessalonians 5:23, Hebrews 4:12). Some beings may exist as spirits without necessarily having a visible body, such as angels and demons (Luke 9:39, 1 John 4:1-3).

Synagogue

In addition to the Temple in Jerusalem, there were numerous locations known as synagogues: consecrated spaces that can be used only for the purpose of prayer and worship. Corporate worship can be carried out only when ten male Jews—a *minyan*—assemble.

Talent

A measure of weight or mass; also a measure of currency. Some scholars calculate the talent in the parables to be equivalent to twenty years of wages for the common worker. Other scholars estimate more conservatively, valuing the New Testament talent somewhere between $1,000 to $30,000.

Temple

The Temple served both as a social gathering place in Jerusalem with a large "Court of the Gentiles," as well as the religious center of Judaism with its inner "Holy of Holies," considered the dwelling place of God. In the "Court of the Priests" animal sacrifices were offered on the altar for forgiveness of sins, psalms were chanted, and prayers offered.

Tithe

Under the Law of Moses, it meant to give one-tenth of one's income to God's work on earth. Jesus teaches that all belongs to God and that while the law demands 10 percent of our goods, Jesus wants all our time, talents and treasure under his lordship.

Other books by James N. Watkins
Characters
Communicate to Change Lives
Should a Christian Wear Purple Sweat Socks?
Squeezing Good Out of Bad
The Why Files: Are There Really Ghosts?
The Why Files: Is There Really Life After Death
The Why Files: When Can I Start Dating?
Writing with Banana Peels

Browse and buy at jameswatkins.com